The Bipolar Relationship

The Bipolar Relationship

How to understand, help, and love your partner

JON P. BLOCH, PHD,
BERNARD GOLDEN, PHD,
AND NANCY ROSENFELD

adamsmedia
Avon, Massachusetts

Published by
Adams Media, a division of F+W Media, Inc.
57 Littlefield Street, Avon, MA 02322. U.S.A.
www.adamsmedia.com

ISBN 10: 1-59869-967-9
ISBN13: 978-1-59869-967-8

Printed in the United States of America.

J I H G F E D C B A

Library of Congress Cataloging-in-Publication Data
is available from the publisher.

To the forces of Love and Patience

Acknowledgments

Thanks to Chelsea King of Adams Media; my agent, June Clark, of FinePrint Literary Management; and Peter Rubie, thereof.

Table of Contents

Introduction

Bipolar disorder doesn't just affect the person who has it. As the person who loves and cares for your bipolar partner, it also affects you. This book has been written with you in mind, to offer you knowledge and skills to assist you in your long-term relationship and to provide you with increased self-understanding and self-compassion. While there is no magic wand to make the entire problem go away, there are very specific actions you can take to make life easier for yourself and for your loved ones. For this reason we have come together to help you to more effectively manage the complexities of this task.

Emotions are contagious, especially in our most significant loving relationships. Therefore, even though you're not the one who has been diagnosed with bipolar disorder, you may find yourself experiencing a whirl of shifting emotional states that leave you full of self-doubt and tension. While you may feel energized and experience great pleasure witnessing your partner's moments of unbridled energy and optimism, you may also be made understandably uneasy by the depression, anxiety, or puzzling behavior that may appear at other moments. It is not easy to live with someone whose emotions seem unpredictable, varying at moments from intense excitement accompanied with unrealistic optimism to severe immobilizing depression.

A major task in any loving relationship involves engaging in compromise for the better of the relationship while at the same time maintaining a sense of one's own identity. This may seem especially difficult when loving someone with bipolar disorder. Loving and caring for a partner with this illness can be extremely rewarding, but it may also push you to your limits of compassion and self-compassion.

A relationship with someone who has bipolar disorder forces you all to recognize what is "normal" or "healthy" and "constructive" or "destructive." If it is in your nature to embrace optimism, you may have difficulty discerning when your partner is unrealistically optimistic. If you are uncomfortable with depressive thoughts you may even feel uneasy when your partner experiences depression. You'll learn how to deal with some of these challenges we address them throughout the book.

It is especially important to remember that you are two adults in a relationship, and that not every difficulty you face as a couple is the "fault" of bipolar disorder. All relationships have problems, and the acceptance of bipolar disorder is an important step toward the realization that we all are human beings living within the parameters of the awareness and skills we currently possess. This greater sense of maturity also involves the knowledge that we can strive to do better and the recognition and acceptance that every relationship requires commitment, compassion, and work.

First and foremost, as the partner of someone who lives with bipolar disorder it is essential to take good care of "you" by paying close attention to your own needs and desires. Self-compassion leads to a healthy partnership.

Your sustained mental and physical well-being will enable you to feel more compassionate and more supportive of your loved one. Should you at any time feel worn down by the strain of your relationship, you may want to seek professional guidance. *The Bipolar Relationship* provides ways of achieving a more fulfilling connection between partners by offering helpful suggestions to you, the caregiver, while you also protect yourself.

PART I

UNDERSTANDING BIPOLAR DISORDER

Fostering a rewarding relationship with your partner begins with understanding the nature of bipolar disorder. In this section, you'll learn what bipolar is, the variety of symptoms that may be associated with it, the forms of bipolar disorder, and current views on what may cause this illness. Additionally, you'll learn some common risks and situations to avoid that may exacerbate or precipitate episodes of the illness.

We share this knowledge to help you foster realistic expectations regarding your partner and your relationship. Living with bipolar illness is a major challenge and learning facts about this disorder is an essential first step in meeting this challenge.

Chapter 1
What You Need to Know

You've picked up this book because the person you love has bipolar illness. By doing so, you demonstrate deep compassion and commitment in your desire to provide the best possible support for your partner, yourself, and the relationship. But, before we go further, let's clear up a few misconceptions:

- There is no shame in loving a person with bipolar disorder.
- It is not your fault your partner has bipolar disorder.
- It is not your partner's fault he has bipolar disorder.
- You cannot "fix" your bipolar partner.

But what you *can* do—and you've taken the first step here—is arm yourself with information that will help you better understand what your partner is going through and weather the rocky times in your relationship. Every couple has their issues, but you are not a typical couple. You face unique challenges and they will be explored. It is important to remember that many people who live with bipolar disorder do not always exhibit symptoms of the illness. At times you will feel just like any other couple with all the usual ups and downs.

What Is Bipolar Disorder?

Bipolar disorder is an illness that is biological in origin and affects moods, judgment, and behavior. Formerly called "manic depression," bipolar disorder involves mood swings that are out of proportion to what is going on in one's life and that vary from intense mania to depression. While everyone experiences ups and downs related to happiness, sadness, and anger, bipolar disorder is marked by the intensity of these reactions. And, while these episodes may follow a life stress, they may persist long after the stressful experiences has been resolved. In general, mania may be characterized by heightened energy, optimism, and activity; depression may include feelings of hopelessness and helplessness, constriction in emotions, and fatigue. (We offer a more complete detailed description of these symptoms in the next section.) Although this illness is related to chemical changes in the brain and is viewed as being influenced by genetic factors, some people still falsely assume the cause is a moral or character flaw.

Many misconceptions exist about this illness, due in part to the media, which frequently focuses on individuals who demonstrate the most severe symptoms of this disorder. For example, they report on actors who appear disorganized and incoherent in their speech; others, who demonstrate drastic and inconsistent changes in their behavior and appearance; and, still others who act in ways that endanger themselves or others. Similarly, the media repeatedly describes criminal behavior as influenced by bipolar illness. However, while some people exhibit extreme symptoms, most do not. The reality is that many who live with bipolar illness are highly successful individuals, both in their relationships and in their work. People in every walk of life—many of whom are extremely creative, interesting, and have achieved great heights in their field—live with bipolar illness. In fact, individuals with bipolar illness often demonstrate a high level of energy and passion for life that can be appealing and contagious. In particular, their manic episodes can easily be misinterpreted as what the French refer to as *joie de vivre* (joy of life). Your bipolar partner may at times seem the most dynamic, talented, and fun-loving person you've ever known.

ASK THE DOCTOR

What celebrities lived with bipolar disorder?

Numerous sources indicate that many prominent individuals have led successful lives despite having bipolar or mood disorders, including: Dick Cavett (television journalist), Richard Dreyfuss (actor), Patty Duke (actress), Connie Francis (singer), Peter Gabriel (musician), Kay Redfield Jamison (psychologist/writer), Patrick J. Kennedy (politician), Ben Stiller (actor), and Ted Turner (entrepreneur).

However, if you love and care about someone who suffers from bipolar illness, it is important to understand the symptoms that he lives with and to realize that these symptoms are reflective of some underlying problem. Like most illnesses, bipolar disorder is beyond the control of the person afflicted. People don't "ask" to be bipolar, nor do they "reinvent" themselves in that way. It is this point to which we will return again and again—that a person cannot wish away his bipolar disorder, nor can someone else will it away.

What Are the Symptoms?

Bipolar disorder exists along a continuum. No two individuals experience the same symptoms, nor does anyone experience them 24-7. Some people go days, weeks, months, or years without an "episode," the period of time during which someone exhibits major symptoms of the illness. Depending on the severity of their bipolar condition, some people will handle the episodes more easily than others. Your ability to recognize these symptoms can aid significantly in the appropriate diagnosis and treatment of a loved one and may also help to reduce the potentially negative impact on your relationship. The following descriptions highlight the variety of symptoms that may be associated with the extreme mood swings from mania to depression inherent to those who suffer from bipolar disorder.

Mania

Mania often begins with a pleasurable sense of increased energy, creativity, and social ease. However, people with mania lack insight and become extremely defensive when others point out a problem. A manic state may be evidenced when your partner has some or all of the following symptoms for at least one week and they interfere with normal functioning:

Manic thinking: A grandiose belief that one is much more than he is. In this state of mind, people can become highly sensitive to criticism or evidence a flight of ideas, moving from topic to topic.

Rapid speech: A pattern of speech that is sometimes so fast the listener cannot follow. The spokesperson may also speak in rhymes, for the mere sake of rhyming, or utter seemingly nonsensical observations like someone high on drugs.

High energy: The inability to slow down, sometimes accompanied by insomnia and the reduced need for sleep. Intense concentration on some activity might give way to extreme impatience. Your partner may also experience accelerated psychomotor activity, the increase in rapid bodily activity that is triggered by mental changes.

Euphoria: An intense sense of well-being, as if nothing bad could possibly occur. This can lead to serious lapses in judgment, unrealistic optimism, and inflated self-confidence. Your bipolar partner may also embark on new projects and make excessive purchases.

Manic psychosis: An extreme form of manic thinking in which people might hear voices or experience delusions about how "great" they are. This can trigger paranoia because the individual is convinced that others are plotting against her out of jealousy.

Risk-taking: Engaging in activities such as impulsively taking trips, forming shaky business investments, dangerous gambling, giving away personal possessions, running up huge bills, and inviting arrest for inappropriate public behavior.

Compulsive sexual activity: Mania can lead to the seeking of a sexual liaison with a total stranger—who may even be dangerous—as well as a total disregard for protection before engaging in physical intimacy. Vows of fidelity are easily discarded during a manic episode. Even when your partner turns to you for his own needs, he may ultimately exhaust you or perhaps encourage you to try something unsafe or outside your comfort zone.

Depression

The shift to depression may arise suddenly and with no apparent trigger. These moods can last for minutes, hours, days, or months. Some symptoms of depression include:

Extreme pessimism: Very depressed people with bipolar disorder may feel easily defeated and frequently lack the capacity to understand why they should keep active. Listless and lethargic, they have difficulty making decisions about even the smallest things. A deep sadness surrounds them, and they may sob for extended periods of time. Because they believe that all efforts lead to failure, bipolar individuals may also try to talk others out of doing things.

Suicidal thoughts: People suffering from depression may believe life is very painful and not worth living. The feeling of unworthiness becomes so pervasive that death may seem the single viable option. Even if suicide is not attempted, depressed bipolar people may be strongly attracted to matters pertaining to death and dying. Even a news story about someone dying may fill a depressed individual with envy rather than sorrow. Highly suicidal people may even appear re-energized before ending their lives, and those observing might even think the person was "getting better" when, in fact, they were relieved that their life would soon end.

Hypomania

The relatively minor manic episodes observed in bipolar II (discussed later in this chapter) are frequently referred to as hypomania. Instead of feeling euphoric, a person suffering a hypomanic episode experiences only heightened confidence. They may lack any trace of doubt or reservations, and may even feel oddly in tune with life, almost as if they know exactly what to say or do. Such attributes may be misconstrued as aspects of their personality rather than a sign of an illness that requires treatment, which further compounds the difficulty in arriving at a diagnosis.

This rush of confidence that your partner may feel can just as suddenly disappear. Anyone meeting your partner for the first time, while he is the "life of the party," might be baffled at the level of social discomfort he displays once back to his former state of "normalcy."

Different Types of Bipolar Disorder

Bipolar disorder is an "umbrella" term used to define multiple types and/or the degree of bipolar illness. Specifically, the *Diagnostic and Statistical Manual of Mental Disorders* lists bipolar I disorder, bipolar II disorder, schizoaffective disorder, bipolar type, bipolar disorder NOS (not otherwise specified), and cyclothymia.

Bipolar I

Individuals with bipolar I illness evidence the most severe symptoms of mania and depression but tend to display more manic symptoms. They may exhibit extreme agitation, grandiosity, or psychotic processing (characterized by difficulties in distinguishing reality from fantasy). Many individuals with bipolar I may require hospitalization, as they evidence impaired judgment, impulsive behavior, and a general lack of understanding regarding their illness. These sufferers are often the least receptive to treatment. They frequently experience several manic episodes, which are then followed by a plunge into depression.

CASE STUDY: James

James, a nineteen-year-old, provides a clear example of someone with bipolar I illness. Dr. Bernard Golden first met with James in a psychiatric inpatient unit. Police had petitioned the courts for James's hospitalization following an incident at the city's major university. While not threatening to harm anyone, James had abruptly entered the reception office of the school's president loudly demanding to meet with the administrator. Before the receptionist could respond, he brazenly walked past her and barged into the president's office, demanding that he be admitted as a student. He ranted loudly and rapidly about his superior qualifications and exclaimed that because he was so bright, he should not have to make a formal application to the program!

His parents were interviewed and detailed James's escalating mania in the weeks prior to the incident. He had slept only a few hours each night for about a week and did not sleep at all the night before appearing on campus. He had become increasingly agitated at home, and in pressured and rapid speech indicated that he should be recognized for his brilliance. His parents reported that he also had spent several days secluded in his room writing but had not shared his work with them. When he finally revealed his thoughts, they focused on his detailed solutions for world peace.

The diagnosis of bipolar I was reflected by his symptoms of mania, his violation of rules (against his history of otherwise appropriate behavior; meaning he showed no evidence of any personality disorder), his grandiose delusions that he should be accepted without application, and the description of his behaviors leading up to the event. Once stabilized with medication, James was extremely apologetic and confused about what had happened. Fortunately, his capacity to recognize and accept his illness led to a very positive course of treatment.

Bipolar II

Individuals with bipolar II disorder—which is more difficult to diagnose than bipolar I—also evidence many symptoms of mania and depression, but the manic stages tend to be less intense than those seen in patients with bipolar I. Further, since the depressive phase of the illness may be more apparent than the manic phase, the patient may be treated for depression *only* rather than both stages of the illness. Over time, a person with bipolar II can also develop the more serious bipolar I disorder.

Schizoaffective Bipolar Disorder

This severe form of the illness has characteristics of schizophrenia. People with this illness may experience psychotic symptoms (hallucinations or delusions) during the manic or depressed episodes or even after these have subsided. This diagnosis is often difficult to make and relies heavily on a personal or family history.

Bipolar Disorder NOS

Bipolar Disorder NOS (not otherwise specified) includes disorders with bipolar symptoms that do not meet the full criteria for other diagnoses of bipolar disorder. For example, this diagnosis may be used when the duration criteria are not met.

Cylclothymia

Cyclothymia is the least severe form of bipolar illness. Emotions are experienced with intensity and there is a desire to shock or act outrageously and with contempt. People with cyclothymia also experience a more mild form of depression than individuals who live with bipolar I or II. These individuals may be extremely sensitive to substances or medications (including marijuana, alcohol, antidepressants, steroids, and, in some cases, high doses of decongestants), which can potentially precipitate more severe mania.

Subtypes of Bipolar Disorder

In addition to the previous diagnoses, there are also subtypes of the disorder. These include mixed or dysphoric mania, rapid-cycling bipolar disorder, bipolar spectrum disorders, and covert cycling. The presence of specific symptoms and the variation in their frequency, intensity, and duration characterizes each different type of the illness.

Mixed Episode

This often occurs in bipolar I and involves such rapid fluctuation between manic and depressive states that it is experienced as a singular episode. For example, rather than feeling euphoric for days or weeks then inconsolable for another several days or weeks, the person is euphoric for perhaps a matter of minutes before plunging into despair, then euphoric again some moments later.

ASK THE DOCTOR

Are you sure it's bipolar?

It should be emphasized that some other conditions may also produce symptoms similar to bipolar disorder on at least a temporary basis. These include thyroid problems, traumas to the head, brain tumors, epilepsy, later stages of syphilis, eating disorders, and drug abuse. Further, mental conditions such as panic disorder, post-traumatic stress disorder, delusional disorder, and schizoaffective disorder sometimes mimic the symptoms of bipolar disorder.

Mixed or Dysphoric Mania

Mixed or dysphoric mania is a combination of depressive and hypo-to-manic stages that coexist concurrently or alternate regularly throughout a single day. For instance, the individual may feel simultaneously grandiose and suicidal. Mixed mania manifests many of the most dangerous traits associated with mania (or hypomania) and depression. A person in this state is frequently unable to sleep, is depressed and suicidal, and experiences delusions of persecution. He is easily excited and grandiose, quick to panic, easy to anger, and highly agitated. Given both the level of high energy and depression, the individual might plot an elaborate suicide.

Rapid Cycling

Patients experience a minimum of four episodes a year, but each cycle is relatively short lived. Rapid cycling—experienced by upwards of 20 percent of all bipolar patients—is evidenced both by individuals who live with bipolar I and bipolar II but is more frequently associated with bipolar II. The onset of rapid cycling usually concurs with a depressive episode, and during the first few years following a bipolar diagnosis. It afflicts a higher percentage of women then men, and studies suggest that it also may be more common in bipolar patients who are mentally challenged. Additionally, thyroid problems or substance abuse may be associated with the tendency to experience this form of the illness

Covert Cycling

Covert cycling is a bipolar spectrum disorder—a class of disorders that have bipolar features—but most often overlaps with bipolar NOS diagnoses. This disorder is found in some people who have periods of depression following several months of effective treatment with antidepressants only to relapse again. In some cases, such patients may present with a pattern of hyperthymia, periods of mildly elevated mood and increased energy that seem within a normal range.

WORD TO THE WISE

Watch for Hypomania and Hyperthymia

Both hypomania and hyperthymia are sometimes perceived as enviable conditions. Employers may rave about hypomanic employees, and others may crave the positive energy and drive hypomanics exhibit as they respond to life's daily challenges. However, both conditions can ultimately lead to serious depression and severe limitations in being able to cope with life's challenges.

People with hyperthymia are characteristically articulate, witty, and creative. In many ways, their condition is akin to low-level mania—not unlike hypomania, which is considered more within the normal range. One crucial difference is that hyperthymia is not episodic but experienced habitually or long-term, like a "permanent high." Still, like any high, hyperthymia tends to render the individual less grounded in the present moment and inclined to periods of depression. These sufferers radiate self-confidence and self-reliance while seeming to believe that they possess limitless power and abilities. Fearless of being the center of attention, people with hyperthymia thrive on new experiences that promise variety, intrigue, and novelty. Generally, they have multiple interests and grandiose plans for the future. Their openness to what is novel and their uninhibited curiosity serves them well in the creative process.

Recognizing the Signs

Life and personality are vastly complex. At any given time, each of us may briefly exhibit some of the symptoms listed, although, for the most part, they're short lived. Under the influence of alcohol, fatigue, stress, a fever, or a major life change, we may all momentarily experience distinct moments when our emotional brain overrides our rational brain and pushes us to display some of these symptoms. This makes diagnosis challenging and makes your ability to recognize the real signs of the illness at the moment they occur very important.

At times in a loving relationship you may lose perspective of who your partner really is because of the way you would like to perceive her. Remain vigilant when looking for signs of bipolar illness, and focus on being as objective as humanly possible. Self-discipline is a prerequisite, as the task at hand is difficult, particularly when facing your own anxieties and concerns about what may be happening to your loved one. The following descriptions highlight key signs to help you recognize the presence of a bipolar episode.

Behavioral Signs

Bipolar disorder impacts thinking, emotions, and behavior, but you can begin to infer the presence of this disorder primarily by observing specific behavioral signs. Keep in mind that a more complete history is essential before an accurate diagnosis can be made. The behavioral signs you may notice include the following:

Speech patterns: Is your partner talking more rapidly than usual? Is it especially difficult for her to stop talking? Is her voice louder than usual? Is she getting hoarse just by talking? When alone, does your partner feel an uncontrollable urge to telephone, e-mail, or write a letter to someone?

Eating and sleeping: Is your partner eating or sleeping significantly more or less frequently than usual?

Irritability: Is your partner crankier than usual? Are extremely trivial mishaps causing him to overreact? Is he more prone to argue than usual?

Easily threatened: If someone interrupts your partner, or if she does not get her own way, does she respond with paranoia or with anger?

Busy but unproductive: Is your partner doing things with nothing to show for it? Are tasks started and ended abruptly?

Lavishness: Is your partner suddenly spending money excessively, giving more gifts, and/or taking more trips? Is he suddenly living beyond his means and/or encouraging you to do so?

Interference: Is your partner giving people advice whether they want it or not? Is this advice being dispensed with an air of false superiority, as if the listener should be grateful to receive such words of wisdom?

Extra-kind to strangers: Is your partner being exceptionally chatty, generous, overbearing, or nosy with people she barely knows? Are these strangers being asked inappropriate questions, including inquiries into their sex lives or their availability?

Heightened drama: Is your partner acting like a "drama queen"? Does he seem to need to stand out from the crowd in the way of talk, dress, or action? Are his emotions extremely intense;

does your partner appear uncharacteristically happy, sad, or angry?

The Calendar

Observing your partner's changes in behavior over time or noting unusual behavioral traits surrounding important days may provide you with key insights into the presence of bipolar disorder. For example, you may observe that your partner's manic (or depressive) episodes tend to run in cycles. If mania tends to follow depression, you may well come to expect that a manic episode will occur once a spell of depression has passed.

The anniversary of a major negative life event is often a tumultuous time for many individuals. These "anniversaries" may arouse memories regarding a loss, a divorce, or the death of a loved one. While such recollections may stir up a short-lived depressed mood in the nonbipolar person, these same memories may at times provoke mania in your bipolar partner. Such "anniversaries" may include the date of a major episode from the past, conjuring up some lingering emotion not fully dealt with and finally resurfacing.

An anticipated event can be as powerful a trigger for a bipolar episode as an event that has already occurred. For example, your partner with bipolar illness may evidence symptoms whether anticipating a joyous event like a wedding or some dreaded occasion such as an encounter with the IRS.

CASE STUDY: Kate

Kate, a twenty-five-year-old patient, reported that, three years prior to her seeking treatment, her mother had died unexpectedly on the eve of Thanksgiving. Kate stated that for the following two years she had periods of mania leading up to the holiday. She recognized that this was a difficult anniversary period for her and, even during previous therapy treatments, focused on the grief and loss she experienced regarding her mother. Unfortunately, she continued to have these reactions.

Only after further discussion did she come to realize that the holiday also marked a time of year that had precipitated her parents' divorce when she was eight. She had been informed of the pending divorce on Thanksgiving and they were formally divorced shortly after the New Year. The combination of the two losses and the tensions associated with them during the holiday, coupled with the history of episodes at this time of year, had made her more vulnerable to an exacerbation of her illness during this time. The treatment that followed helped her to identify ways to be more proactive in trying to avoid a relapse as the next Thanksgiving approached.

Others' Observations

Besides relying on your observations, symptoms noticed by others may also provide valuable information about the possibility of an impending bipolar episode. Sources of such observations may include:

- *Your partner's doctor:* A trained professional who is qualified to recognize signs that your partner may be on the verge of a manic or depressive episode is an invaluable source.
- *People familiar with your partner's disorder:* Friends, neighbors, and family members, who may share with you or your partner their very real concerns that things may be going in a risky direction. They may point out behaviors they have witnessed and encourage your loved one to see his doctor.
- *People who do not know your partner is bipolar:* These people may comment that something appears to be very wrong. They may also share their discomfort by mentioning the symptoms of mania displayed by your partner or some act or gesture that seemed inappropriate.

Is Bipolar Disorder Genetic?

This is the million-dollar question for those of you who love someone diagnosed with the illness. Unfortunately, the answer is yes—but this "yes" has several disclaimers.

Scientific research supports the theory of a genetic contribution to bipolar disorder. This does not literally mean that Bipolar Person A will automatically give birth to Bipolar Person B. Genetics are much more complicated than that. But there is a tendency for mood disorders in general—bipolar or otherwise—to be shared among first-degree relatives (parents, children, and siblings). Again, this doesn't mean that all first-degree relatives will automatically transmit the bipolar gene.

Increasingly, scientists turn to studies of identical twins to try to solve the riddle of nature versus nurture for any number of human conditions. Research has found that identical twins are more likely to share a mood disorder than fraternal twins. This would seem to give additional credence to the notion that mood disorders are one of many genetically transmitted traits. Still, even with identical twins, it is not a 100 percent certainty that both twins will carry the bipolar gene.

We need to point out that research has increasingly emphasized the role environmental factors play in modifying the potential influence of genes. For example, research indicates that while a potential range of intelligence may be influenced by our genetic makeup, our actual intelligence will be strongly influenced by whether or not environmental factors support and nurture our intelligence. Similarly, someone may have the innate ability to play the piano, but if she is never offered the opportunity to play, her talent will never be realized.

A genetic predisposition to bipolar or other mood disorders may also be more likely to manifest during certain life experiences. For example, recreational drug use can heighten the possibility of some mood disorders as the brain struggles to cope with all the extra stimulation. Also, while traumatic experiences can trigger mood imbalances in anyone, the difference between someone with a mood disorder and someone without one can be the ability to psychologically sort through these experiences rather than being completely overwhelmed by them. However, sometimes bipolar symptoms can appear seemingly out of nowhere, with nothing traumatic to trigger them.

The Causes

While the causes of bipolar disorder are still being discovered, there are several key factors that are increasingly being identified as contributing to this illness.

Many studies have endeavored to identify processes in the brain, that may occur for those with bipolar illness and that are significantly different without this disorder. Much of this research has centered on neurotransmitters, chemicals that carry messages between cells or between cells and muscles. Neurotransmitters frequently work extremely quickly. For example, when you voluntarily lift your arm, there is a rapid-fire message going from your brain to your arm muscles saying, "Lift." Different neurotransmitters in the brain are responsible for different kinds of messages. For example:

- **Serotonin** helps to modulate such things as mood, anger, appetite, sleep, and sexual impulses.
- **Dopamine** is also associated with mood and sleep, as well as motivation and reward, learning, attention, sociability, and cognition (how the brain identifies what it experiences).
- **Norepinephrine** is both a neurotransmitter and hormone that impacts one's ability to pay attention and respond, mood, hypotension, heart rate, and fight-or-flight response (the impulse of the body processes to either flee or attack when faced with danger).

Research on bipolar disorder often has explored the possibility of there being too many or too few neurotransmitters in a given individual's brain. Other research has considered the possibility that different neurotransmitters must achieve the proper balance in relation to each other—that the problem is with the brain cells themselves, which are too sensitive or not sensitive enough in their response to neurotransmitters. Some researchers also have considered the possibility that more brain cells exist in people with bipolar disorder, again, dealing with the common notion that too much or not enough of something exists in the brain.

WORD TO THE WISE

Load Up on Serotonin

Serotonin can be raised by the foods we eat: certain kinds of mushrooms, fruits, vegetables, high-carb foods such as grains, and sugary candies. Still, foods contain many other natural chemicals that can counteract the intake of serotonin, so diet alone will not make or break severe mood swings.

The human brain has been studied only as far as our technology to date will take us. For example, some kinds of brain research cannot yet be performed on the living. Yet, while different studies might reach somewhat different conclusions as to the causes of bipolar disorder, we do know that the medications (described in Chapter 3) are based on this research and seek to right or balance the processes and chemicals of the brain. And, with substantial percentages of people responding to these medications, it would appear we're on the right track.

Some people find great comfort in this research, which informs them that all mood swings are symptoms of the illness. They buy into the notion that we cannot alter what takes place in the brain.

Yet, some people are frightened to learn that their illness may be caused by something that went "wrong" with their brains. Others think that human beings are more than the sum of their parts, and that their soul—the very essence of their being—is able to transcend chemicals, body parts, and synapses. So it may be disheartening to your bipolar partner to consider that people are only what our brain chemistry permits us to be.

Your views on this issue may greatly impact, either negatively or positively, the role you play in helping your partner obtain appropriate treatment. We encourage you to be mindful of continuous research that focuses on identifying new causes and treatments for managing the symptoms of bipolar disorder. All regimens are designed to reduce—or even eliminate—a patient's symptoms, the objective being to help your partner lead a more fulfilling and productive life. A major aspect of this goal is to become more familiar with the specific needs of your partner and the ways in which his illness is expressed. Toward this end, we highlight how bipolar is different for each individual in the next chapter.

Chapter 2
Bipolar Is Different for Each Individual

The life journey is different for every individual diagnosed with bipolar disorder. It would be reassuring to know that your loved one will lead a successful life and be maximally available to engage in a loving relationship, and one with minimal hardship. Unfortunately, life has no guarantees and no one can predict the future.

Being a "bipolar person" can suggest many things about your partner. If you rigidly adhere to a blueprint about how relationships and your partner "should" be, you will ultimately be setting yourself up for disappointment, tension, and hurt. Conversely, if you strive to develop your resilience—including flexibility and patience—you will feel increasingly comforted by the expanding variety of treatments that have made this illness more manageable.

Depression

In a severe depression, your partner may not want to leave the comfort of home or do anything. You may need to attend that much-anticipated social event alone or even cancel vacation plans.

It may even be difficult for you to enjoy a television show, knowing your partner is alone and brooding in another room.

Other times you may feel grief and concern for your depressed partner and may experience frustration over your inability to be of help. Your partner may even reject your hugs and caresses, which can feel like the ultimate form of rejection. At other times you may find yourself losing patience and resent your partner for making your own life feel oppressive and gloomy. You may feel a sense of guilt if something makes you laugh. You may even begin to wonder: "What about me? I sometimes get depressed, too. Is this relationship worth it?" Don't worry though. It's natural to wonder about your ability to continue in a bipolar relationship.

A key factor in coping with your partner's depression is the ability to not personalize her withdrawal. Depression is anchored in self-absorption and involves a sense of helplessness and hopelessness that can frequently encompass self-loathing. It causes constriction in thought, emotion, and physical activity, and it limits connections with others. Therefore, it's very important that you address your own needs by making time for relaxation and recreation and by maintaining your social supports and connections. While self-compassion fuels your energy and overall capacity to remain concerned for your loved one, neglecting yourself may only fuel resentment and antagonism.

Always remember that many episodes are single occurrences, transient rather than grounded in permanency, like periodic storms in an otherwise favorable climate.

Eating and Sleeping

Two very basic human needs—food and sleep—can become major issues when you live with a bipolar person. For differing reasons, both mania and depression can make some people disinclined to eat and/or sleep. Others respond to depression with an increased desire to eat and sleep. While all of us need to stay healthy by eating properly and getting sufficient rest, such concerns are even more important for the bipolar person. If your partner is not eating well, or if she is getting insufficient rest, this may indicate an episode is brewing. Forgoing food and sleep can either be a cause or a symptom. Either way, you must deal with the fact and do your best to cope with these conditions as you remain vigilant about your own eating and sleeping requirements.

If you force your partner to eat or sleep, he may accuse you of being a control freak or a nag. Your actions may also boomerang, as mental conditions are often fearless in the face of criticism. On the other hand, if you say or do nothing, your loved one's condition may worsen. If your partner cannot sleep—and if sleeping aids are not part of the medication regime—remind her that simply lying still with closed eyes provides some rest and is better than nothing. This may trigger a regular routine for sleeping.

Likewise, although balanced meals are the ideal, if your partner will only eat hot dogs and French fries three times daily, it's better than the alternative of starvation. If you feel it's necessary, seek professional intervention by contacting your partner's physician.

Imaginary Aches and Pains

It can be difficult to discern whether or not the pain being complained about is real or imaginary since after a period of time it's like "crying wolf." You may inadvertently dismiss something significant or believe you are wasting time over what you perceive to be a made-up ache or pain. Like most humans, you may grow weary about multiple complaints over seemingly minor issues.

Such aches and pains may also seem to occur at the most inopportune times, like during a special evening out or while on vacation. At such times it is helpful to remember that bipolar disorder is an illness of extremes. You partner may experience the pain of a sprained ankle as rating a 7 on a pain intensity scale of 1 to 10 (with 10 being severe). This cannot be considered an imaginary pain, but rather a preoccupation with physical ailments and discomfort due in part to the cluster of symptoms that define depression. While trying to remain empathic may be challenging, your desire to "fix" the pain may lead to further frustration. The better route: express concern, assess the nature of the pain, inquire what you can do, and act accordingly. Your partner may only expect you to listen, not solve the problem.

Limited Concentration

Whether the result of bipolar symptoms, certain medications, or both, you may discover your loved one's inability to concentrate on anything for long periods of time. Your partner may abruptly change the subject when you're speaking or may lack the attention span needed to complete even the simplest household chore. Even reading a newspaper article you hoped to discuss together may seem like a burden for your partner—leading to more frustration for you! Although some bipolar people respond well to their medications, for others concentration is an issue that can be discouraging to the partner who feels ignored.

You might want to address your partner's lack of concentration by engaging in face-to-face conversation rather than attempting to talk across the room or between rooms. It may be helpful to summarize what you have discussed, especially if your conversation contained a plan that involves some follow-through. Forming lists together and providing visual cues, flash cards, or motivational posters can help prompt mindfulness. While these are effective measures, always maintain realistic expectations regarding their impact, especially when your partner is in the middle of an episode.

Rapid Speech

When your partner is manic and the attempt at conversation is an effort, you may feel unable to even interject a word every now and then. In the throes of mania, your partner may speak so rapidly and forcefully that the word "conversation" no longer applies. During the course of rapid speech—referred to as a monologue—the *art* of diplomacy can fly right out the window at the expense of hurt feelings. Rapid speech can also accelerate into high drama and even violent gestures. It's important that you realize that you may not be getting through to your partner, as rapid speech often reflects the whirling thoughts that are symptomatic of mania.

At low levels of rapid speech, gently providing feedback about your inability to follow your partner's end of the conversation may yield a positive response. Similarly, you may share your observation that such behavior may reflect an escalating intensity of mania.

Extreme Arrogance

Your partner may suddenly develop an extremely inflated sense of who he is and say or do things that others interpret as rude or egomaniac—if not delusional. For example, if your partner is playing solitaire and you suggest he put the black ten on the red jack, the response might be volatile and frustrating: "Don't tell me how to play, because I've been playing this game for years and am much better than you!"

In reaction to your perceived need to justify your comments you may try to convince your partner of the reality of the situation. But, any attempt to justify your comments could lead to an escalation of tension focused on your different perceptions of the reality. An alternative response is to share how you feel emotionally impacted—hurt, devalued, or attacked—by his words. A sharing of feelings is more constructive than venting pent-up anger and disappointment.

While sharing your feelings, be realistic about your partner's capacity to comprehend and answer appropriately. The very ability to freely express yourself, whether or not your partner responds, may ease your frustration. At the very least, the release of bottled-up feelings averts any further disappointment and resentment. Being the target of someone's grandiose accusations can trigger any insecurities you may have and leave you vulnerable. Still, even though it can be difficult to remember, be mindful that such responses say more about your partner's illness than your own strength and weakness.

Inappropriate Anger

All of us lose our temper at times, and even over things that later appear trivial. It frequently is the proverbial straw that breaks the camel's back. All in the same day your boss criticizes you, you got stuck in traffic, you return home and accidentally break a glass, and then you explode in the loss of control.

Your bipolar partner may overreact to something out of nowhere. The two of you could be enjoying a perfectly nice dinner until, suddenly, one of your partner's peas falls off his plate and he loses it. He starts yelling at you for making peas when you know he has trouble eating them . . . and on and on.

Being the target of a partner's anger can be extremely unsettling in any relationship, but it is even more challenging when the anger is expressed by your partner with bipolar disorder. You may react with feelings of sadness, disappointment, frustration, confusion, helplessness, or even your own feelings of anger. You may also experience a sense of betrayal as you perceive your loved one as having broken an alliance—the cherished bond you have vowed to uphold. Such moments may test your capacity for compassion and empathy.

It is understandable that many of the symptoms may lead you to feel alienated and even experience your loved one as your adversary rather than your ally in a loving relationship. The intensity of mania or depression only furthers these reactions when you feel powerless to connect—especially when your partner is angry. Enduring such episodes requires you to be mindful that emotions are contagious and reacting with similar anger will only further exacerbate the difficulty of the moment.

At such an impasse, remind yourself that your loved one is held hostage by her emotions. Your best response is the same you may have for a screaming child. Inch close by, unless it exacerbates her reaction. Encourage her to sit in the most comfortable chair in the room, a way of helping to diminish body tension. If you are having any impact at all, the lowering of your voice and the slowing of your speech may help calm your angry partner. If you think you're getting through, share how you feel impacted. You may even want to sit it out if the situation remains at a verbal level. Conversely, if your partner is out of control you should state your limits and seek help if you're fearful about her harming herself or you.

Overly Meddlesome

It is hard for many of us to mind our own business, but someone in the throes of a manic episode may take things to the extreme. Maybe you mention that your boss doesn't appreciate you taking long lunches, and your bipolar partner reacts by doing you a "favor." He calls your boss on your behalf, explaining how you should be able to take all the time you need. Or maybe someone your partner does not even know—a friend of a friend, or a movie star—becomes an obsession. She tells her neighbor to inform his nephew that he must go to college, or maybe even finds the nephew's phone number and tells him herself even if they've never met. Maybe your partner writes a letter to a movie star, telling her she must leave her no-good husband, and then continues an endless stream of letters to her. Your partner's target may experience this as stalking, even though he is not physically in pursuit of the celebrity, nor does he think they are destined to be lovers. Yet needless time and energy, which could better be spent constructively, is wasted on minding everyone else's business.

It is understandable that such behavior could provoke discomfort when publicly aired. While you may find it embarrassing, be mindful that you cannot control the actions of others. Your distress is likely triggered by many factors. For instance, you may feel uncomfortable for your loved one—or ashamed, if you believe that your partner's behavior reflects on your inability to help manage her illness. Or, you may feel vulnerable to the opinion of others regarding your very choice of a partner. Any interference into the privacy of a relationship may be challenged when boundaries are crossed.

Since your partner may not be in a position to hear you now, wait for the most opportune time to gently provide feedback about how she affects others and their perception of her. You can frame your comments by emphasizing her good intentions, while reminding her how she might feel if others were to be similarly intrusive by instructing her how to live her life.

Sexual Compulsion

It goes without saying that a healthy sex life can help a couple stay together, but it can be devastating to the union if one of the partners is in sexual overdrive. For example, consider the woman with an overactive libido who pleads with her partner to stay in bed rather than get up and go to work. Or, the sex-maniac who hungers for physical stimulation all night and won't let his partner get any sleep.

Sexual compulsiveness also leads to promiscuity. While some people may be unfaithful in any relationship, during a manic episode your mate may be compulsively driven to engage in sexual activity with you and others during the same time period. This uncontrollable yearning for excitement is coupled with the physical and emotional rush that accompanies physical intimacy.

In today's world, sexual promiscuity can lead to unprotected sex, which places both of your lives in jeopardy. It can also lead to an unplanned pregnancy with someone outside of your relationship. Regardless of the reasons for your partner's promiscuity, such behavior may push you to the limits of your commitment. Remember, safety first! If you are uncomfortable with the way your partner is treating you, say something.

Similarly, be alert to the uneasiness you may experience if you are violating your own boundaries regarding physical intimacy. While caught up by the emotions that accompany a manic episode, your partner may request that you experiment in the sexual arena. Although some novelty can add spice to your romantic life, everyone deserves the right to define their own limits regarding sexual experimentation. If discussion doesn't seem to help, you may want to seek professional help. This may involve your own individual therapy to deal with your reactions and to explore helpful strategies for your unique situation. Couples therapy, where both of you can be helped to share concerns and learn how to rebuild trust, may also be beneficial.

Irrational Risk-Taking

Taking risks can add excitement to life and test your courage—provided, of course, that they are "appropriate" risks. For example, if you've always wanted to take up rock climbing, you would likely sign up with a professional trainer and learn how to do it right. But someone who is suffering from mania may claim to know how to rock climb without ever having tried it and just set out on his own.

Not only might this person risk physical danger, but financial risks may also be involved. Excessive gambling, investments you cannot afford (or are unlikely to pay off), or even refusing to comply with legal advice in some crucial matter, believing the judge will rule in his favor if he presents that perfect speech he wrote himself, fall under this category. Such inappropriate risks are unlikely to succeed and may cause major problems for you and your partner.

Risk-taking at this level calls for assertive intervention. Trying to reason with your partner at such times may be futile and leave him vulnerable to his impulses. Moreover, you'll be confronted with the task of trying to maintain your overall well-being and that of your partner. This may include confiscating credit cards, hiding checkbooks, and taking control of finances. The situation may pose great conflict for you, but the alternative of financial havoc is much worse. While your effort to discourage your partner from engaging in risky situations may work at times, you may also need to elicit the help of others—a relative, a neighbor, or even the police—especially when the perceived risk poses physical danger or may be life threatening.

Chapter 3
Forms of Treatment

Bipolar disorder is a chronic illness that requires ongoing monitoring and management. While alternative forms of therapy are continuously identified as beneficial, research supports the view that medication therapy is the primary treatment for good management and that psychotherapy is the most positive complimentary form of treatment. Still, for many individuals, full engagement in psychotherapy is dependent on some minimal level of symptomatic stabilization that only medication can promote.

As the partner to someone with bipolar disorder, you play an influential role in determining your mate's choice of and engagement in treatment—especially medication therapy. While no cures exist for this disorder, staying informed and helping your partner seek and practice the most appropriate treatments can help reduce, ward off, and even eliminate the most chaotic and crippling symptoms that accompany this illness.

Your partner, like many individuals with this disorder, may be reluctant to accept medication therapy because of common concerns and fear. As your own views may support or reduce her uneasiness, be mindful that she may need to explore similar fears as you establish your personal attitudes regarding medication treatment. For example, your partner may fear the loss of those euphoric feelings associated with unrealistic optimism or that medication will diminish her energy, productivity, and creativity. She may even be concerned that she'll be controlled by the medication and lose her autonomy and capacity to control her own emotions, thoughts, and behaviors. For many, their fears are a powerful deterrent to medication management.

Partners often struggle to come to terms about treatment. As the nonbipolar partner, we encourage you to recognize that the goals of medicine and psychotherapy are to help your partner live a life that more fully reflects her "real" self. When working effectively, medications and therapy can help reduce the impact of those emotional states that override and interfere with constructive thoughts and behaviors.

Medications

Recent breakthroughs in medication have minimized the effects of bipolar disorder. These new medications are targeted to the individual symptoms of the illness rather than all symptoms. For this reason, medication management usually includes more than one choice of remedy.

A wide range of responses to medication exists, from eliminating symptoms to not relieving any—and everything in between. Sometimes a given medication may become less effective over time or its effect will change when it is combined with a new medication. As a partner, you have the unique opportunity to be alert to these changes. While you may be pleased with the apparent stabilization for your partner as the result of some particular medication regimen, the impact may diminish. This may be due to the medications or to some exacerbation of the illness experienced by your partner.

It's important to remember that medications may still have side effects even when working properly. While common side effects may be irritating, the benefits in most cases outweigh the discomfort. We encourage you to check with your partner's doctor or pharmacist about potential side effects before your partner begins taking them (and you should certainly obtain permission to do so). Sudden changes should not be minimized nor neglected and must be immediately reported to the physician.

Mood Stabilizers

Initially, the FDA approved lithium, Depakote, and Zyprexa as mood stabilizers, but other medications have since received approval. Additionally, some medications are used for bipolar symptoms that are not officially approved specifically for the disorder but are FDA approved.

- **Lithium**, on the market since the 1970s, has been one of the most frequently prescribed medications to inhibit mood swings. While primarily used to stop mania, it has also been shown to help prevent a recurrence of manic and/or depressive episodes. If your partner is prescribed lithium, it is recommended that she have regular blood tests to rule out its impact on the kidneys or thyroid. Another caution—since lithium is a salt, it can be dangerous for someone who is on a low-sodium diet.
- **Valproate (Depakote)** is an anticonvulsant that has also been found to be effective in the treatment of bipolar disorder. It's particularly effective with mania and useful for acute and long-term treatment, helping reduce the intensity of mood swings.
- **Carbamazepine (Atretol and Tegretol)** was originally developed as an anticonvulsant, but it works well on acute mania—especially with patients who experience rapid cycling, or mixed episodes.

- **Antiepileptic drugs (AED)**, such as Lamictal, are found to be effective supplements in the treatment of bipolar illness when they are administered with other medications.
- **Antipsychotics**, originally developed for the treatment of schizophrenia, are another effective medication for bipolar management. The first generation of antipsychotics ("typical antipsychotics") is effective in the treatment of bipolar illness that evidences psychosis. Second-generation antipsychotics ("atypical antipsychotics"), a more effective regimen for psychosis with fewer accompanying side effects, are also used to manage nonpsychotic bipolar disorder. These drugs include risperidone (Risperdal), olanzapine (Zyprexa), quetiapine (Seroquel), ziprasidone (Geodon), and aripiprazole (Abilify). The latter two medications help reduce mood instability and anxiety with less sedative impact.

WORD TO THE WISE:
Treatments Are Often Accidental

Mood stabilizers are frequently discovered by accident. Lithium was first used as a dissolving agent for another substance that researchers had hoped would be effective in mood stabilizing. Most current medications were first developed for the treatment of epilepsy.

Certain mood stabilizers should be avoided during pregnancy. Lithium has been associated with a slightly increased rate of congenital heart defects. Depakote, Tegretol, and other anticonvulsants have been linked with serious defects to an infant's nervous system.

Antidepressants

While most research on antidepressants has focused on unipolar depression, these medications have increasingly been used to also treat bipolar illness. However, a major concern in the use of antidepressants with bipolar patients is their potential to trigger manic symptoms. This makes a correct bipolar diagnosis and the need to supplement mood-regulating medications to counter potential manic episodes extremely important.

Some of the common side effects associated with antidepressants include drowsiness, sedation, headaches, agitation, dry mouth, insomnia, impotence or other sexual dysfunction, nausea, and gastrointestinal problems. Three classes of medications are most often prescribed for depression:

- **Selective serotonin reuptake inhibitors (SSRIs)**, which include: Prozac, Zoloft, and Paxil, are accompanied by few side effects and a low likelihood of triggering mania. SSRIs keep serotonin—a neurotransmitter, released by nerve endings in the brain and associated with mood and depression—from being reabsorbed by nerve cells after transmitting its impulse, thereby enabling the brain to receive and use more serotonin.
- **Monoamine oxidase inhibitors (MAOI)** were often prescribed prior to the discovery of SSRIs. These, however, have more side effects and require a strict diet because of their interactions with certain foods and medications.
- **Newer antidepressants** work at least as well as SSRIs, and with a minimum of side effects. Wellbutrin works on dopamine and norepinephrine, two neurotransmitters, and is less likely than other antidepressants to produce mania. Effexor acts more quickly than most antidepressants, and is less associated with sexual problems. Cymbalta and Remeron impact two neurotransmitter systems and have been effective for patients who have not been helped with other forms of antidepressants.

Antianxiety Drugs and Sleep Aids

Antianxiety drugs are useful in episodes of relatively minor anxiety and help patients sleep. They are also an effective regimen for people who aren't bipolar, but these drugs should be prescribed with caution since some can be addictive.

- **Benzodiazepines,** such as Valium, Librium, Xanax, Activan, and Halcion, are highly addictive and may trigger drowsiness and memory loss. Patients taking benzodiazepines are prone to diminished inhibitions and extreme behavior, including suicide, and should be administered these drugs only on a short-term basis as a supplemental treatment for acute mania.
- **Hypnotics,** such as Ambien and Sonata, can lead to memory impairment and other cognitive functions—even hallucinations. Withdrawal symptoms include seizures, increased heart rate, nausea, abdominal cramps, tremors, and anxiety. We emphasize that these drugs are prescribed *only* for short-term or sporadic usage so the patient does not become dependent on them.

ASK THE DOCTOR

Will my partner have to change medication frequently?

In today's world, the majority of bipolar patients will make at least one switch in medical treatment at some point during their therapy, especially since newer medications continue to be developed that promise better treatment.

Medical Checkups

Although no cure has been found for bipolar disorder, the expanded development of medications has helped to make it an increasingly more manageable illness. With commitment, persis-

Signal Hill Library
Self Checkout

01:02 PM 2016/08/15

---

1. The bipolar relationship : how to understand, help, and love your partner
39065107015503 Due: 9/6/2016,23:59

Total 1 item(s).

To check your card and renew items
go to www.calgarylibrary.ca
or call 262-2928

tence, and patience, you and your partner can work together with your partner's doctor to identify the medications that work best. It's important that both of you pay close attention to what seems to be working and what does not.

Medication therapy for bipolar disorder must be checked regularly for physical responses, and this requires professional testing since some changes may not be detectable to the layperson. Testing may include assessment of your partner's blood count, urine, thyroid, and electrolytes before and after prescribing a mood stabilizer. Regular follow-ups are also important to ensure all medications are being used at safe levels and that interaction with other meds is not causing problems. Since bipolar disorder is usually treated with multiple drugs it is important to note any physiological changes that occur.

WORD TO THE WISE

Avoid Recreational Drugs

Bipolar disorder is far from being the only cause of delusions and paranoia. Even relatively mild recreational drugs, like marijuana, can trigger these conditions in anyone but would probably exacerbate bipolar symptoms in your partner.

The Third Wheel in Your Relationship

When you love someone who is bipolar, the best-case scenario is that your loved one follows a medication routine that produces few if any side effects and enables him to lead a normal life without others suspecting something is seriously wrong. While this is the reality for some couples, for others the issue of medication is more complex. Sometimes the issue of medication is like a third wheel in the relationship; it seems as though a day cannot go by without medication being a source of contention.

Your own views on the subject of medication may influence the frequency of such conflicts if your partner maintains a contrary position. For example, if your partner has a negative attitude regarding medication and you hold an opposing view, conflict may arise when you suggest he take his meds. Tension and conflict may also arise if your partner feels that you are downplaying the disturbing side effects of the medication.

"Many" Does Not Mean "All"

It's important to remember that although medication therapy relieves painful symptoms for many people, "many" does not mean "all." If your partner claims to have no response to the meds, it can be true. Conversely, your partner could be in denial of her illness and resistant to care. Your partner may also lack a clear sense of how others see her—and what feels "normal" to her may not be seen as "normal" behavior to others. Since other people have no idea what's really going on with your partner, whether or not she follows through with a medical regimen can lead to inner turmoil both for your partner and for those who interact with her. As the significant other, your own sense of how well the medication is working might play a major role in discussions of treatment.

Going Off Medication

Be aware that once your partner feels stabilized, it's natural for him to think that he no longer needs medication because he feels "fine." But, going off his meds can lead to serious problems as old behaviors return. Your once happy life together may seem to begin to fall apart as the daring of mania and/or the lethargy of depression seems to rule your relationship—and your life.

If your partner does choose to stop taking his medication, you are likely to worry and may even wonder if you should remain in the relationship. Unfortunately, it's legally close to impossible to force someone to take medication and there may be little you can do in this situation.

Finding the Right Combination

Since bipolar disorder is a multifaceted illness, your partner will probably be prescribed more than one medication, and calculating the right dosage takes time. Although some patients may experience immediate relief, others will find only partial relief from their symptoms. Your partner may engage in a kind of trade-off, deciding (for example) to live with feeling listless if it means avoiding severe mania.

WORD TO THE WISE

Use "I" Statements

It often is tempting to say to another person, "You are sloppy" or, "You drive me crazy." However, studies reveal that people respond better to "I" statements—declarations that emphasize how you are impacted rather than your thoughts or feelings about your partner. For example, you might say, "I don't appreciate having to pick up your pajamas off the floor" or, "I get scared when you don't eat or sleep." In this way, you're communicating your discontent about certain things rather than instructing your partner on what to do.

Depending on the quality and strength of your relationship, you may have a lot of influence about your loved one's medication issues or you may be completely shut out. Helpful suggestions can be perceived as nagging or interference, but silence can be unfair to you and your loved one who could benefit from your constructive input. Since to err is human, you undoubtedly will say or do the wrong thing at least once when it comes to your loved one's medication. You may remind her once too often to take her meds, or perhaps "helpfully" point out some side effect you are noticing and end up hurting her feelings.

"I Don't Believe in Medication"

If you do not believe in medication treatment, you may advocate that a healthy lifestyle or a strong spiritual foundation is all your partner needs. Even some psychiatrists are hesitant to prescribe medications and instead advocate the use of other kinds of therapy. However, while living a healthy, spiritual life may be good for everyone, risking somebody else's life—especially an individual with a history of destructive behavior—by encouraging him to ignore prescribed medical treatment is irresponsible albeit well-intentioned.

CASE STUDY: Jane

Dr. Golden remembers being very opposed to any use of medication for treatment. Both in his early training, which had a psychoanalytic underpinning, and as part of his confidence in the human spirit, he believed that other approaches could be equally effective even with alleviating severe psychological symptoms. It was with this perspective that he first met Jane, an attractive thirty-eight-year-old woman in a psychiatric hospital. She had been admitted following an altercation with her landlord. He had come by to inspect her apartment but had been informed by neighbors that the typically reserved high school art teacher had seemed increasingly argumentative and had begun to turn up the volume on her stereo during the late hours of the night. The landlord found Jane's apartment to be in complete disarray, with rooms full of newspapers and magazines scattered around the floors and piled high on furniture. Paintings and paint supplies were also observed throughout the apartment with blotches of paint on the walls and floor. Additionally, several half-finished murals were discovered painted on her walls.

Dr. Golden met with Jane just a few moments following her admission. With intense passion she spoke loudly and boastfully of her history as an artist who had had gallery showings in New York. She said that she had in recent years taken a break so that she could work on her art. She was disheveled in appearance and claimed that she was awaiting a check for $10,000 that she would use to pay her rent and move to another apartment.

Dr. Golden remembers being taken in by Jane's bohemian appearance and admiring her passion and intensity, the flare to her language, and the excitement in her face and voice. While he and other staff were not fully convinced of her success, they were all immediately interested in finding out more about her and strongly hoped that her story was true.

Jane was administered medications for several days before being stabilized, and Dr. Golden remembers feeling disappointment and sadness while meeting with her a week later. She appeared subdued in her tone, the twinkle in her eye was greatly diminished, and she no longer spoke of her dreams for greater artistic success. Jane's doctors later learned that, while Jane was very artistic, she had never had any gallery showings.

Based on this and many other experiences, Dr. Golden realized that medications were a necessary part of treatment and that not using medication only leads to further suffering for many patients. He gradually came to realize that when medications are really working, they can effectively help individuals become more true to themselves rather than muting who they are.

Psychotherapy

In recent years, the combination of medication and psychotherapy has become the favored treatment approach for many mental health care providers. Psychotherapy addresses a variety of concerns regarding bipolar illness and helps patients manage and reduce depression. Additionally, psychotherapy helps patients successfully master the phases of mourning and grief that foster acceptance of the diagnosis. Such mourning involves letting go of one's beliefs regarding how life "should" be while gradually recognizing and accepting the limitations that may accompany the illness. The ability to accomplish this task reflects emotional maturity, which is significant for anyone managing a chronic illness. By going through this process your partner can more fully accept that she is not her illness, but instead lives with a bipolar diagnosis.

Continued therapy can help your partner address such common issues as, "I do not have this illness" (denial), "This should not be happening to me" (anger), and "I will never be able to have a good life" (depression). A process of mourning can help your partner become more fully self-compassionate in recognizing, acknowledging, and addressing her needs.

It is important for you to remember that your partner has a personality separate and distinct from her disorder, which includes a composite of traits, beliefs, and attitudes that define who she is. How she typically reacts to life challenges, her capacity for resilience, and her emotional intelligence are just a few aspects of her personality that will shape her views and whether she is able to accept her diagnosis and treatment. Psychotherapy can help her develop more effective responses to life challenges while enhancing her resilience. Similarly, she can learn emotional intelligence, which includes the ability to calm herself, identify her emotions, and be empathic with others, all of which will impact how she manages her illness.

The most effective forms of complementary treatments in psychotherapy include the following therapies.

Cognitive Behavioral Therapy

Cognitive behavioral therapy (CBT) is one of the most widely used and researched forms of therapy and is highly effective in dealing with depression. Patients are helped to reduce and eliminate any thoughts related to depression by identifying distortions in their thinking, then challenging and replacing them. Specifically, they are helped to address and replace self-critical thoughts that reflect helplessness and hopelessness. For example, a client who states "I am a failure" regarding a specific task may be helped to remind himself that "I just did not have the information I needed" or "I had unrealistically high self-expectations about how I should have performed." In recent years this approach has also been expanded and integrated into other techniques.

Behavioral Activation Therapy

Behavioral activation therapy (BAT) emphasizes how behavior contributes to mood. For example, your partner may be helped to focus on the outcome of her behavior when facing the choice between getting up or remaining in bed. BAT will help her recognize and anticipate the impact of her actions—that completing a few small tasks around the house will more positively influence her mood than remaining in bed. Moreover, your partner will learn to view depression as something that encompasses only specific moments—considered approach-avoidance conflicts—in life. Such moments are guided by the therapist whose task is to help the patient define an action in which the motivation to act outweighs the tendencies associated with depression.

Acceptance and Commitment Therapy

Acceptance and commitment therapy (ACT) helps patients cope with depression by integrating a broad variety of theories regarding psychopathology and change. A major premise of this approach is that change begins with the acceptance of a person's reactions, that is, their emotions, thoughts, images, and bodily responses. The goal is to observe these reactions without judgment rather than feeling compelled to act or deny them. ACT emphasizes how little control we have over the arousal of these reactions and also helps patients identify personal values that can serve as guidelines for living. Patients are urged to examine their behavior in terms of how their actions help bring them closer to achieving their goals.

Mindfulness-Based Cognitive Therapy

Mindfulness-based cognitive therapy (MBCT) is a form of psychotherapy that attempts to reduce a possible relapse in recurrent depression. It is offered as part of maintenance psychotherapy rather than during an acute phase of depression. Exercises in mindfulness involve helping patients experience and increase their ability to heed their internal experiences without responding to them. For example, mindfulness can help your partner calm his mind while more comfortably addressing his thoughts, emotions, and sensations that may be negative in content. This process will help your partner view these experiences as not defining who he is.

Family-Focused Treatment

Family-focused treatment (FFT) is an effective approach to help bipolar patients and their families and is frequently offered in hospital settings. This approach involves groups of families who are taught communication skills such as active listening, offering one another feedback, and framing requests in a positive manner. FFT is viewed as an effective measure in reducing relapse and hospitalization as compared to individual treatment alone.

Some therapies focus predominantly on teaching coping skills and helping patients alter their responses to the negative impact of events. For example, your partner may be helped to respond to stress in the workplace by learning relaxation skills, better forms of communication, and the art of assertiveness. The goal is not to eliminate your partner's reactions but to lessen their intensity, longevity, and pervasiveness.

Problem-Solving Therapy

Learning specific problem-solving skills may also be a beneficial approach for your partner. Problem-solving therapy focuses on helping people identify, discover, or invent ways of coping with specific problems of daily living. It also involves learning ways to monitor actions and to correct them if needed. Learning such skills is proactive in focus and may be most appropriate during times when your partner is stable or experiencing only mild depression or mania.

Psychotherapeutic approaches emphasize that while your partner's illness may originate from a biological predisposition, she can have great impact on her response to the illness and how she manages it. Most importantly, these approaches highlight your partner's ability to judge and evaluate her illness, thereby playing a significant role in determining the course of her illness.

There Is No "Happy Pill" for Couples

When your partner's life and, by extension, your life is consumed with medication and therapy, the temptation to believe in pills for everything (including happiness) is very real. Life brings with it ups and downs and each of us faces disappointment, loss, and hurt that are a natural consequence of fully embracing life. While you may sometimes crave a "happy pill," there is nothing out there that guarantees a happy relationship.

Does Bipolar Come First?

It should be emphasized that, from your partner's point of view, managing bipolar symptoms is an accomplishment unto itself. We all tend to think in this way at least some of the time. Anyone, bipolar or not, may think: "I kept my baby clean and fed today, so nothing else matters." Or, "I finished the Jones account at work, so nothing else matters." Nobody can pay equal attention to all things all the time. In fact, entire days, weeks, or months may pass in which your bipolar partner (like any flawed human being) feels the need to concentrate on managing his symptoms at the expense of other pursuits, like you.

WORD TO THE WISE

Enjoy Your Partner

Studies illustrate that couples who stay together and happily cohabitate are the ones who genuinely enjoy each other's company and share strong bonds of trust. Do you trust your bipolar partner? Do you genuinely enjoy her company? These are questions only you can answer.

Many people in relationships report one or both partners focusing on things other than the relationship at any given time. While this does not automatically assume the relationship is in trouble, at some point both partners must address their personal and shared needs as a couple. Since life is filled with distractions, it is essential to create some balance in your life while you patiently wait for your partner to be more available to you. You must experience a rewarding life beyond your relationship and any worry about your partner, such as an enjoyable career, community involvement, personal hobbies, or friends. Balance is a key ingredient for any healthy relationship.

Stability Can Be Deceptive

If bipolar disorder seems at times to dominate your relationship, the opposite may also exist. You forget that your partner is bipolar because the symptoms are under control and you have little reason to focus on them until some unexpected episode occurs that shocks you back to reality. Even if you've been through this before, if the problem manifests at some inopportune moment—your son's piano recital, or during your presentation at work—you may feel as though the rug has been pulled out from under you. At such moments, it can be difficult to remember that your partner is not having a bipolar episode on purpose. It may even feel planned, especially if he "always" seems to act out at the most inconvenient time.

At such moments, you may want to view your partner's episodes as passing storms in an overall positive climate by being mindful of all the good times when problems did not present. By journaling or using a calendar to note days of greater stability, you can recognize such episodes as fleeting disturbances rather than long protracted periods of confrontation.

Sometimes it is easy to forget about your partner's bipolar disorder, even when you seem to wrestle with symptoms on a regular basis. The bipolar issue becomes so integrated into your daily routine that it is not uncommon to stop thinking about it. Many people with physical disabilities, and even their loved ones, will acknowledge their adjustment to the disability and take it for granted as part of their lives.

Nevertheless, mental issues are seldom treated with the same compassion as physical ones, which explains how you may overlook your partner's out-of-control bipolar symptoms. However, try not to be too hard on yourself for losing patience when bipolar symptoms unexpectedly erupt. Everyone is guilty of "losing it" from time to time! Always keep in mind that you're dealing with an illness.

The Shared Challenge of Being Human

Bipolar disorder is a serious condition like any other critical illness, and your loved one—like you and the rest of humanity—has weaknesses and flaws. Although some bipolar patients have difficulty functioning, are periodically hospitalized, or live on disability, it's a mistake to blame all of your relationship problems on bipolar disorder, especially if your bipolar loved one capably handles such everyday tasks as holding down a job and/or parenting.

You and your partner both bring your share of problems to the relationship, and each of you has issues or situations that require patience and understanding in return. Even when bipolar symptoms are under control, your partner might annoy you for forgetting to buy something for dinner, or his snoring may annoy you. Coping with bipolar disorder does not entitle you to more rights than your partner. Remember: your loved one never asked to be bipolar.

ASK THE DOCTOR

Does it matter if I react more to big or little problems?

Sometimes a relationship with someone with bipolar illness ends over major problems: your partner goes to prison, or loses your life savings, or gets pregnant by somebody else. However, many people react more calmly to the big challenges and become more upset over small things. It is the more minor challenges of everyday life that more frequently erode the bonds of a loving relationship.

Bipolar disorder is also a very human condition, and one that plagues people with a wide range of symptoms. To grasp this concept more fully, consider a particular action and amplify it beyond a manageable range. However, remember that the feelings themselves—both depression and euphoria—are not unlike emotions periodically experienced by all of us. By underscoring your shared humanity through attitudes and actions, you can best support an enduring relationship with your partner; such compassion and self-compassion is the foundation for any successful relationship.

Chapter 4
Addressing Differences and Maintaining Realistic Expectations

Let's make one thing clear—all relationships come with inherent risk. While relationships usually begin with both people putting their best foot forward, they soon progress past that honeymoon stage—sometimes in a positive direction, other times with turmoil. Sometimes an increased sense of openness can reveal differences that may stand in contrast to your deeply held convictions. Attitudes regarding money, religion, how much time to spend together and how to spend that time are among the issues that need addressing. Even when a relationship does not suffer from severe hardship, the partners may still experience trying moments. Although many of us can relate to the usual day-to-day hassles that accompany cohabitation, sometimes these "hassles" can blossom into irreconcilable differences.

Statistics confirm that up to 50 percent of all marriages in the United States end in divorce. By contrast, studies suggest the divorce rate can reach the 90 percentile for couples in which one partner is bipolar. Yet, despite these grim statistics, it's important to remember that for *any* relationship to survive both parties must accept the bitter with the sweet, the good times with the bad. When it comes to loving a person with bipolar disorder, you're agreeing to take on additional risk by learning to recognize the signs and mitigate the impact of the disorder on your relationship. Let's look at some ways to help you manage the risks involved.

What's the Risk Factor?

How much risk is inherent in a bipolar relationship? Should you end it before giving it a chance? Not necessarily. Remember, when someone responds well to medication, living with this person will be no different than living with anyone else. You will have good times and bad times, and even if the relationship fails it may be for reasons unrelated to bipolar disorder.

You may feel compassionate to the struggles of a bipolar person who is wrestling to find a medication regime that works. Your partner must decide, with the help of professional guidance, how to balance one medication with another one, or if the side effects of a third medication are worth undertaking. Take, for example, individuals who say it is hard to accomplish certain tasks when on their meds. They feel their medication dulls their senses, and although they no longer suffer extreme ups and downs, neither do they feel much of anything. Their emotions feel "muted," and they report a diminished sense of being fully present with the events of their day. Consequently, before any important exam or a stage performance or even writing a book—remember that creativity and bipolar go hand-in-hand—people with bipolar disorder frequently go off their meds because they feel that the medication inhibits their creativity. Others might be fed up with the need to keep track of so many daily pills, and still others experience difficulty in the morning and may have trouble maintaining employment that requires early hours. In moving forward with your relationship, you may conclude that the positives outweigh the challenges of loving a partner with bipolar illness. As in any relationship, we all face difficulties, and it ultimately is up to each individual to determine by an evaluation of criteria whether or not the commitment is worth the effort.

For some, living with a partner who is dangerous to herself or others may be the final hurdle that leads them to seriously question their commitment.

Not everyone shares the same capacity for dealing with the imperfections of life. If you are short on patience, if an orderly existence is a high priority, if you don't like surprises or being interrupted, or if you adhere to a strict financial budget and feel wary of problems, don't worry! None of these issues mean you're a bad person, but they may indicate that life with a bipolar person is not for you. If you are in this position and losing sleep over potential future problems with your partner, now is the time to recognize your limitations and be proactive.

A partnership with someone who has mental illness can feel overwhelming. But, you're not alone. Support groups, which we will discuss in more depth later, exist throughout the country for family and friends who have loved ones with bipolar disorder. You may also want to seek counseling for yourself to help strengthen your capacity for commitment in a bipolar relationship. It is also helpful to read books like this and keep them nearby to refer to periodically when questions or problems arise. Ultimately, only you can determine your limitations and what may be in your own best interest.

Balance and a Healthy Relationship

A healthy relationship, one in which each partner experiences mutual respect, caring, recognition, and responsibility, involves balance. Many relationships experience tension as the balance shifts.

One partner may assert too much responsibility for decision-making and may instruct his loved one on how to behave. A shift in balance may be the outcome of one partner attempting to dominate the relationship, but it may also occur when one partner is unavailable or unwilling to carry her weight. This often happens when one partner is physically ill for a short period of time. However, living with a partner who has bipolar disorder presents a long-term challenge to maintaining balance.

Each of you may feel resentment when the shift of balance is significant. You may resent the amount of energy it takes to help your partner manage her bipolar disorder. You may also feel resentful if your needs for closeness and sharing are not satisfied. At the same time your partner may develop resentment based on her illness and her inability to carry her weight in the relationship. She may also harbor resentment over your constant reminders about how to live her life. This imbalance can lead to your partner feeling childlike and ultimately viewing you as a controlling parent. Unfortunately, since the illness encompasses the emotions over rational thinking, you may be obliged to assume the role of a parent. This leads both partners to feel great frustration and ultimately undermines the stability of the relationship.

While the urge to care for your partner is understandable, be mindful that your attempts to "fix" him will not work. You cannot fix a "normal" relationship, and bipolar relationships present greater challenges. Some common roles you may find yourself falling into include the following:

The Reprogrammer

Some people think they can reprogram their loved one into not being bipolar. Not unlike a dog trainer, the reprogrammer assumes the responsibility of teaching the bipolar partner different behavioral and cognitive responses. "Time out and take a deep breath," this partner may say to her loved one. "Is this really worth getting so excited about?" The reprogrammer may even "helpfully" use a highlighting pen in the checkbook to remind the bipolar person to update the balance when writing a check.

Whereas people can change old patterns of thinking and behavior, this requires discipline, commitment, a strong motivation to change, and practice. In addition, it frequently requires professional guidance or the employment of long-proven techniques such as those previously described in Chapter 3. Because of this, even in a nonbipolar context, efforts to change another person are likely to fail. People do not change unwillingly, and they need to experience such change as a choice they're making for themselves and in the way they determine it to happen. Despite all good intentions and beliefs that your approach is the most suitable, your partner needs to do it his way. In part, this reflects your partner's need to experience control over his life. Additionally, if he seeks change, the nature of that change and the degree of commitment must resonate with your partner. By playing the role of reprogrammer, you foster resentment. Remember, it's human nature to want to live our own lives and make our own mistakes. Although your partner's decisions may not coincide with your timelines or preferred approach, and may even cause added frustration, they serve as another reminder to always maintain realistic expectations regarding your capacity to implement change.

Be mindful that your tendency to play reprogammer may be strongly influenced by your own unrealistic expectations of your loved one. Such expectations may be fueled by your own perfectionism and the need to be perceived as correct. Rigidly maintaining the expectation that your partner *should* be or act in a certain manner will only foster unnecessary anxiety, anger, and hurt.

CASE STUDY: Kelly and Raymond

Kelly was a devoted partner who believed she could effectively help her husband, Raymond, meet any challenge he faced as a result of his bipolar illness. Raymond, a highly successful computer graphics designer, had been diagnosed three years into their relationship. As a result, their relationship was impacted for several years by his periods of mania and depression. Raymond's strong sense of stigma concerning his diagnosis often led to him to refuse to take his medications and resulted in a general lack of commitment to treatment.

Kelly, the oldest of four children, had long ago embraced the caretaker role in her family and continued that now with Raymond. Increasingly, she became more involved in assuming responsibility for not just supporting his efforts, but also for making sure he took better care of himself. Kelly wrote notes on Post-its and strategically placed them throughout the house in an effort to remind Raymond to take his medications, follow a routine, and be attentive to the slightest indication that he was entering a period of mania. She rigorously tried to set a routine for bedtime, when to eat, and to include a social life that she thought would be conducive to his stability. She scheduled Raymond's appointments for blood level tests and attended support groups to learn about the illness while he remained at home.

As Kelly took on added responsibility she simultaneously lowered her expectations for Raymond while elevating her own so she could be more effective in getting him to assume responsibility. Despite the intensity of her commitment to change her partner, Kelly became increasingly self-critical as Raymond only minimally engaged in his own self-care.

Kelly sought counseling when her efforts had culminated in a variety of stress symptoms including anxiety, insomnia, and impaired concentration. In treatment she learned to adjust the expectations of herself and her mate, and as a result was better able to recognize and accept that, while she could help her husband in many ways, it was ultimately his responsibility to be more engaged in his own treatment.

The Health Guru

A healthy diet, exercise, and fresh air are good choices for anyone and, if you're in a bipolar relationship, both you and your partner will benefit from these choices. Similarly, it will be helpful for you to be alert to foods or additives that may impact mood. For example, excessive amounts of caffeine and sugar should be avoided, but the rule of thumb is to take everything in moderation.

As a society, we have been slow to embrace a healthy lifestyle. People with bipolar disorder are not the only ones who binge on candy bars and greasy chips, nor are they unique to fanatically staying in shape at the expense of putting themselves in harm's way. So if you find yourself thinking "If only my bipolar partner would take more vitamins and stop eating cheeseburgers, everything would be okay," you may want to think again. If he enjoys exercise and healthy food, that is great. But expecting him or her to never fall prey to junk food is setting an expectation for your partner that millions of others—many of whom are well-organized and disciplined in other ways—can't meet. Although well intended, your overzealous expectations may further exacerbate your partner's tension and add to any existing conflicts in your relationship.

The Magician

When all else fails, you may think magic is the answer—*poof*, and with the flick of a wand your problems fritter away. You want to believe that your loved one can miraculously be cured, but the role of the magician exists largely in your mind. Perhaps you keep your thoughts to yourself, not even admitting these fantasies to your partner. Yet, when you and your partner embrace you find yourself thinking, "It will all go away, I just know it."

When your partner's condition does not disappear as you willed it, you pull another kind of disappearing act called denial. As illogical as it may be, you convince yourself that what happened was destined to occur. You may try to pretend it's not real or convince yourself that it was some strange misunderstanding that will fade away.

Playing the role of magician reflects a form of denial wherein you are fooling yourself into thinking you're in control over what—in reality—you have no control over. Your challenge as a partner is to distinguish reality from make-believe if you are to help manage your partner's illness. This may require some degree of mourning as you go through the process of grieving what you perceive as your failure to control.

Reasons for and Consequences of Denial

Many risks exist when you engage in denial regarding your partner's bipolar condition or the seriousness of it. Such risks include the inability to recognize the symptoms of an impending episode—either manic or depressive. Denial may also lead to a delay in seeking treatment. For example, you may encourage or ignore a drinking binge while your partner is on medications. In your effort to deny or minimize her condition, you may even engage in activities that interfere with her healthy sleep routine. There are many reasons why someone might engage in this extreme form of denial, including the following.

Love

It may be hurtful to grasp that your mate is suffering a serious illness. The basic tendency is to believe it is all a mistake, and if you wish hard enough the diagnosis will fade away much like a bad dream. As an outgrowth of your love, you want your partner to be healthy and happy. However, the way to help her achieve this goal involves a wide range of strategies. Bipolar illness is complex and calls for a variety of approaches, including medication, lifestyle changes, psychotherapy, education, the help of a support group, and continuous support from family and friends. While your love may be profoundly deep, you cannot deny the long-term nature of bipolar illness.

"Workaholic" Society

We live in a time and place in which people are expected to lead increasingly active lives. Foreign visitors frequently comment on our strong work ethics, and studies reveal that Americans work longer and harder than most people from other countries. Although the "new normal" defines Americans as a people who never slow down, it is important to differentiate this from mania that goes beyond the norm, as the manic individual can cause real harm to himself and/or others.

Creativity and Bipolar Disorder

Since creativity and the arts go hand-in-hand, a wide range of celebrities live with bipolar disorder. Yet, their very popularity and success belies the stress and suffering under which bipolar sufferers live. Since their success may derive from episodes of manic energy, the tendency is to overlook the intense struggle that these celebrities face when severely depressed.

Since bipolar disorder is often associated with creativity, it is not unusual for people in the arts to go off their medication—both temporarily or permanently—to maintain a high level of creative output without the inhibiting side affects of medication therapy. As the partner of a bipolar person, you may think of your loved one as "full of life" or "very talented," anything but bipolar. And even if your bipolar loved one is neither an artist nor an intellectual, he may still share common characteristics—such as intensity and a "larger than life" personality—with his famous counterparts. These individuals, renowned or otherwise, can be highly temperamental and prone to sudden fits of anger and despair. Not only are they vulnerable to self-inflicted injury, but it can also be scary to be in their company.

Bipolar Disorder Is "Only" Mental

A common assumption is that mental conditions are imagined since, unlike a broken leg, mental illness is hidden from view. Some individuals even maintain the misconception that mental illness—because of its very nature and invisibility—can simply vanish if we will it away. You may also be harboring a sense of unreality, not fully accepting that your partner's bipolar diagnosis is for real. If medication therapy is controlling the symptoms, it may be unnecessary for others to know about your partner's condition. That which is kept secret often seems less "real" than what is shared.

Societal Stigma

A powerful motivating force that may foster your denial is the "stigma" associated with mental illness. While our society has come a long way—through public education, the "coming out" of successful individuals with mental illness, and the work of advocacy groups—stigma continues to exist. Such perceived shame, which is most frequently based on fear and lack of knowledge, can be a powerful deterrent to recognizing and appropriately addressing your partner's needs and challenges.

Although potential risks exist in any bipolar relationship and may, at times, feel overwhelming, there is reason for optimism. In the next chapter we provide an expanded discussion of coping strategies to help you reduce the impact of an impending risk.

Embracing these strategies as part of your repertoire will take commitment, patience, and practice, but you'll learn specific ways to enhance your resilience and subsequent optimism when dealing with the challenges of loving your partner.

Chapter 5
What to Avoid

While bipolar disorder is rooted in genetics and no foolproof way exists of keeping it at bay, certain situations are more likely to trigger an episode. Like a faulty thermostat that leads to unstable temperatures in your home, bipolar disorder may leave your partner vulnerable to even the slightest change of stressors. These may include the demands of work, the expectations she maintains of herself and others, changes in diet and the quality of sleep, any change of routine or medications, financial challenges, and personal relationships, including the one you share with each other.

High-Stress Activities

While everyone has to deal with stress, your bipolar partner faces special challenges. He is more vulnerable to mood shifts, lacks self-calming skills, and is prone to develop adverse side effects from medication changes. Besides a poor self-image and discomfort regarding his diagnosis, the amount of energy required to monitor stress—even moderate levels of stress—may be destabilizing for your partner. When dealing with bipolar disorder, no setting should be considered a zone of comfort and calm. At the same time, some key situations have greater potential to heighten stress and trigger bipolar episodes.

People to Avoid

Anyone who seems to interfere with your partner's treatment should be avoided whenever possible. The prescribed treatment is between the patient and her doctor, and you—to the extent that the doctor feels it appropriate to share. No interference should be tolerated, even from well-intentioned relatives and close friends.

Intrusiveness can be very troubling, especially if you or your partner is already ambivalent about the form of treatment being used. Besides, meddling may exacerbate your partner's sense of shame or failure. She may be particularly sensitive about having to take medication, viewing it as a reflection of some weakness in her character. Any interference can be an unfair and stressful burden to place on your partner, who may feel undue pressure to explain and justify her decisions.

ASK THE DOCTOR

Who advocates for bipolar individuals?

Oftentimes individuals with bipolar disorder who have more fully accepted their illness and are secure with their decisions are the one's to inform the public about the benefits of medication therapy and other effective coping strategies. These frequently are the people who become the most vocal advocates in helping to reduce the stigma of mental illness.

You can be a real source of help to your partner. By discussing the situation with her, you can help determine her level of comfort in sharing with others how she feels about her their interference. Perhaps she'll want you to join her in confronting family members, or she may even prefer that you speak with them alone. If your partner is in the middle of an episode, it may be in the interest of both of you to immediately level with family. Either you or your partner can tactfully thank them for their interest and good intentions, but let them know that based on your knowledge, the two of you have decided on the chosen course of treatment. If you sense any resistance, emphasize how their interference is impacting both of you. Ultimately, you may find it necessary to firmly set limits about what they can and cannot discuss, and even the amount of time you spend with them.

Other people to avoid include:

- ***Negative acquaintances:*** Some acquaintances will offer positive reinforcement, expressing warmth and affection in ways that are healthy and in your partner's best interest. By contrast, others may seek out your partner for reasons that reflect negative traits. Their primary motive may be camaraderie, but accepting it is neither in your or your partner's best interest, as the relationship may intensify your partner's stress level.
- ***Substance abusers:*** Someone with bipolar disorder who demonstrates erratic or destructive behavior may unwittingly attract others who behave similarly. For example, someone with an alcohol or substance abuse problem may be attracted to your partner when he is caught up by the emotions of an episode. This person's attraction to the emotionality of mania may echo a personal need for impulsiveness, excessive optimism, eccentricity, and even risk-taking. Caution also applies to people with other types of addictions or compulsions, such as gambling or sex.
- ***People with untreated mood disorders:*** Be wary of people with mood disorders who are not receiving any form of treatment.

This includes people with eating and sleeping disorders who are not in therapy and people with apparent mood disorders who have never been diagnosed. Any of these behaviors can negatively influence your partner.

- ***Fanatics:*** Be mindful of people with obsessive, fanatical traits, like the person whose hobby has taken over his life. Someone whose politics are so extreme that they join lunatic fringe groups or advocate the elimination of an entire group of people may excite the manic side of a bipolar person who is inclined to have a quick change of opinion. Religious groups that claim to be the one and only *true* religion and isolate themselves from people of other faiths can also attract the vulnerable bipolar individual.
- ***Criminals:*** Although nobody should associate with criminals, bipolar individuals can more easily be harmed if connected in any way with a criminal mind. High rollers in the financial market and those who routinely lose lots of money through faulty investments are also bad companions.
- ***Gossips:*** Most of us are guilty of occasional gossiping, but a person who seems to get a rush by talking against others should be shunned. This type of personality is often linked with manic grandiosity.
- ***Needy people:*** Very needy people are also bad influences. Someone in need of money or who is embroiled in a serious emotional crisis can spark arrogance or empathy "gone awry" in your bipolar partner. The next thing you know, your partner is emptying the bank account and spending too much time away from home.
- ***Prejudiced people:*** Be alert to those who seem prejudiced to bipolar disorder or those who may tolerate your bipolar partner out of pity, a feeling of superiority, or perhaps because she lacks other friends. Chances are this person is not a real friend and is best avoided.

Jobs

People like or dislike their chosen occupation for a variety of reasons that may include financial compensation, camaraderie with fellow employees, workload, the boss, the commute, and even the actual physical environment. In the best of situations a job is equally rewarding in all areas, but dissatisfaction in one or more areas can cause anxiety.

For the bipolar person, job-related situations can lead to extreme stress and trigger manic or depressive episodes. Your partner may not just hate her boss; she may be unable to stop thinking about him. Perhaps your partner's job seems pointless and makes him depressed. Perhaps, in the throes of manic grandiosity, your partner believes that her work is unworthy of her and that she should be rich and famous rather than working side-by-side with inferior individuals.

Even people who obtain their highest professional aspirations can sometimes suffer. Bipolar or not, top executives endure health problems or premature death because of too much stress. Many top athletes and famous movie stars find wealth and fame a burden and resort to drug abuse or even senseless acts of crime. For the bipolar person who achieves her cherished career goal, the same pressures will be encountered . . . but at a heightened level. Even ordinary jobs can be accompanied by looming deadlines, excessive amounts of overtime, irate customers, or many additional factors likely to increase stress.

No "perfect" job exists for the bipolar person, but you should ask your bipolar partner the following questions:

- Do you drink more or engage in substance abuse because of upsetting things that happen at work?
- Did you resume smoking after taking the new job?
- Have your eating or sleeping patterns deteriorated since taking on this job?

- Do you regularly wake up in the middle of the night with anxiety over your job?
- Do you find yourself unable to enjoy your time away from work because you cannot stop thinking about it?
- Does your job fill you with anger and rage?
- Do you find yourself wishing for bad things to happen to your fellow employees?
- Does the thought of returning to work make you feel extremely depressed?
- Do you have less of a social life since taking on this job?
- During time off from work, do you want to stay in bed and hide from the world?
- During time off from work, do you want to engage in reckless behavior like binge spending or compulsive sex?

If your partner has answered yes to at least one of these items, she should be encouraged to identify the workplace concerns that contribute to her stress. She may also seek to develop strategies to help manage those pressures. For example, she may consider registering for a seminar to help employees deal with difficult people in the workplace. Or, she might learn coping skills such as problem solving, organization, delegation, assertiveness, and even anxiety and anger management to help her deal more effectively with her unique stress.

ASK THE DOCTOR

What can my partner's employer do to help?

The Office of Disability of the Department of Labor offers recommendations for accommodating a bipolar worker, which include flexible or part-time work, frequent, small breaks, small tasks, and a work environment with few distractions. To learn more, go to *www.dol.gov/odep/welcome.html.*

Based on your partner's new level of proficiency, she may decide to assertively request improved working hours, renegotiate her responsibilities, ask for assistance with her job, or even request a raise. Alternatively, by identifying her specific stressors your partner may decide to maintain her present job while seeking satisfaction elsewhere. For example, she may seek creative outlets in the arts, more supportive social connections, or she may even go back to school to learn new job skills—anything outside the work arena that may add fulfillment to her life.

For many individuals with bipolar illness, finding a way to work from home can be the ideal stress-free situation. It offers increased freedom in time scheduling, not to mention the lack of commute and interpersonal stress. However, this choice requires self-discipline and may be isolating if your partner desires greater social contact.

CASE STUDY: Whitney

Identifying suitable work was a major challenge faced by twenty-eight-year-old Whitney. For several years Whitney was successful in a management position for a retail business. Having great flexibility in her schedule and workload contributed to her favorable performance. It also permitted Whitney to play an active role in her treatment while maintaining a balanced life with her husband, friends, career, and leisure time.

Unfortunately, the demands of Whitney's job abruptly and drastically changed when she was assigned a new supervisor and when a difficult economy led to increased demands of all employees. She experienced heightened anxiety and stress as a result of being required to work longer days and earlier hours. Her sense of harmony, maintained by a balance of activities, was soon impacted by her increased work demands. She found herself more tense and soon experienced sleep difficulties that contributed to the onset of mania. Despite her husband's supportive attitude, a period of depression soon followed. She had become increasingly fatigued, returning home with little energy left to relate to her husband or to attend to the chores of daily living. On weekends, Whitney became more socially withdrawn and spent more time in bed in an effort to both regroup and conserve her energy. She then sought adjustments to her medication and made the decision to terminate her position.

After stabilizing and considering her situation from all points of view, Whitney eventually sought a part-time job to provide some income while she began training for a medical billing position. She continued her job while she established a medical billing service from her home. She had made the decision to work from home in order to have more control over her time and work pressure. While the couple faced many financial challenges for almost a year during the transition, Whitney ultimately gained an increased sense of satisfaction in her work and a greater autonomy that was essential in helping her effectively manage her illness.

Recreational Drugs/Alcohol

Unfortunately, many people who claim to be "social drinkers" in reality indulge too heavily. Some medications prescribed for bipolar patients explicitly warn against the consumption of alcoholic beverages and should be heeded to avoid serious health risks—and even death.

If your bipolar partner is not taking medication, or if none of the medications preclude the use of alcohol, it still is wise to be attentive to even so-called "recreational" or moderate drugging or drinking habits. Remember, bipolar disorder involves mood imbalance and alcohol is a powerful drug with potentially serious consequences regarding mood alterations. Some bipolar patients my even be self-medicating—using drugs or alcohol to diminish negative emotions or to fuel positive ones.

Some signs to watch out for include:

- ***Signs of alcohol abuse*** may include slurred speech, difficulty in self-expression, a sudden lack of coordination, averting eye contact, morning headaches, and lethargy.
- ***Signs of marijuana use*** may include bloodshot eyes, a sudden appetite for snacks, wetting lips or excessive thirst (also known as "cotton mouth"), body odor, and averting eye contact. You may also find paraphernalia, like paper or smoking devices, associated with marijuana usage.
- ***Signs of cocaine or amphetamine use*** may be difficult to distinguish from mania, except that substance abuse may appear shorter in duration. People high on cocaine may seem unusually nervous or restless and ramble on and on in meaningless conversation. If you look closely, their eyes may be dilated even in a well-lit room, and other symptoms such as a runny or bloody nose may be apparent. Periods of abnormal high energy are usually followed by exhaustion and severe depression. Your partner may not want to even get out of bed.
- ***Signs of amphetamine use*** may include mania, shaky hands, restlessness, and rapid speech. Other symptoms include incoherence, hyperactivity, reduced attention span, and periods of sleeplessness followed by periods of "catch-up" sleep.

While alert to signs that your partner may be abusing drugs or alcohol, be mindful to relate to her with the love and sensitivity of one adult to another and not parent to child. Some of the above signs may also resemble certain aspects of bipolar illness, so always be vigilant and don't jump to conclusions. Real signs may include secretive behaviors such as a shift in personality or a sudden drop in work performance. Your partner may stop caring for your home or even withdraw from you and make new acquaintances.

Your feelings about drugs and alcohol will impact how you react to your partner's indulgence. You may, for example, enjoy a drink or two each evening. While this may not be a problem for you, be aware of your partner's history with alcohol. Although she might be capable of handling her alcohol, bipolar patients as a rule are more vulnerable to the negative effects of liquor.

A loving and compassionate approach is usually the best way to encourage your partner to refrain from drugs or alcohol. Articulate your love for her as the person she is, not as the person she becomes in an altered state. You want to communicate your concern about the negative impact of her indulgence and the sense of loss you experience when she loses control. You may even decide to avoid drinking in her company or abstain completely as a way of demonstrating your support.

If your partner does use drugs or abuses alcohol, suggest she seek counseling from a private practitioner or a group like Alcohol Anonymous (AA) and Narcotics Anonymous (NA). Help for yourself is obtainable through a support group like Al-Anon, and couples counseling offers a viable option for the two of you to attend together.

Your partner will hopefully respond positively to your suggestions, but be prepared for her to minimize her problem or refuse outright to address the issue. Dealing with an addictive partner who refuses to seek help is challenging and stresses a relationship, but cohabiting with that addictive partner can be even more challenging. It takes persistence, on your part, while being attentive to your own needs as you determine the best course of action. Whatever your decision, remember there is no right or wrong answer. The outcome is different for every couple.

Gambling Settings

Millions of people enjoy gambling as a recreational activity. For some, buying that one-dollar weekly lottery ticket offers hope for a better tomorrow. Many gamblers win or lose a modest amount of money that they can handle without stress while enjoying the suspense or challenge of the game. However, anyone living with bipolar disorder is more vulnerable to gambling abuse and addiction.

WORD TO THE WISE

Avoid the Urge to Gamble

Anyone experiencing the urge to gamble can call a hotline number twenty-four hours a day, seven days a week, and speak with someone. The United States Gambling Hotline is 1-800-522-4700. The Canadian Gambling Hotline is 1-888-391-1111.

Without behaving like a parent, you can skillfully manage your family's financial situation and remain on the alert for potential gambling binges as a responsible partner of someone with bipolar disorder. Similarly, and without seeming overly intrusive, you may want to monitor your partner's Internet activities to thwart any potential hazard before it becomes a reality and damages your relationship. Your partner may be able to enjoy some form of gambling without problems, but at the same time his motivation to gamble may be heightened in response to the grandiosity, risk-taking, and delusions that accompany a manic episode. Gambling for some people with bipolar disorder can parallel the danger of a child playing with matches. Perhaps nothing bad will happen, but it just might. Since this form of entertainment can be concurrently stimulating and depressing, a winning streak can trigger a rush of self-aggrandizement. Should their winning turn to losing, some people with bipolar may risk staying up all night with the hope of regaining their initial stroke of luck. For others, losing money can produce thoughts of paranoia and despair that ultimately end in suicide.

If gambling becomes a way of life, your bipolar partner is well advised to avoid it altogether. Skip the visits to Las Vegas, where gambling is taken for granted and may be an enticement too great for your bipolar partner. Like flaunting alcohol in front of someone on the wagon, the impact of such a visit may have lasting repercussions. The lure of instant wealth and twenty-four-hour availability, coupled with the encouragement to drink and high excitement, is a potentially volatile or lethal situation for someone with bipolar disorder.

Sexual Settings

Whereas parties and taverns may have historically provided the most frequent settings for people to hook up for a sexual encounter, the Internet has facilitated such meetings. Anyone with computer access can go online to arrange a one-night stand. Regardless of personal views, today's society is increasingly invested in sexual fulfillment. Casual sex, sex without commitment, and sexual intimacy outside the bonds of matrimony are more accepted nowadays.

Whatever your position about sexual issues, for your bipolar partner a rampant sexual spree can mean loss of money and serious physical risk. Your partner can be beaten, or worse, by someone who catches her in bed with his mate. She may also engage in unsafe sex with disastrous consequences, such as contracting a sexually transmitted disease like HIV. These encounters may also include the use of alcohol.

If you expect monogamy, be vigilant. While not every person with bipolar illness is quick to act out sexually, some may be more inclined during a manic episode. As a partner, remaining alert to such actions and the settings that may foster them may help you reduce potential difficulties in your relationship. This is not to suggest that you should fear the worst or that you should force your partner to remain by your side, but you should maintain a cautious awareness to such behavior. Similarly, trust your judgment. If you do suspect your partner is having a tryst, it's better to confront the issue than ignore its possible existence. Communicating how you are impacted by your partner's behavior will underscore the importance of your feelings.

ASK THE DOCTOR
Is sex an "addiction"?

Some professionals would reply affirmatively while others disagree, but everyone agrees that sexual behavior can get out of control and cost loved one's their material possessions and even their lives. However, behaviors associated with "sexual addiction" do not necessarily lead to "sex offences" such as rape and molestation, as deviant behavior involves control issues and other psychological problems that reach beyond sexual matters.

Diminished sexual desire and issues with sexual performance are often side effects of the medications prescribed for bipolar disorder. It is advisable to have serious talks with your partner and her doctor about sex, and then reach an agreement with your partner about the best path for you as a couple. Open discussions about sex—even experimenting within the relationship—may provide your partner answers for any of her concerns.

Abnormal Eating and Sleeping Patterns

You may hear the familiar saying in a twelve-step group, "HALT—are you really upset, or just hungry, angry, lonely, or tired?" If your passion is gourmet food and you enjoy a good night's sleep, you may have difficulty understanding why some people have problems with these basic needs. Nevertheless, bipolar people frequently view eating and sleeping among their major demons.

Not Eating or Sleeping Enough

Lack of eating and sleeping can be associated with mania and depression, those times when a person is too high or too low to eat and sleep. Even if your bipolar partner enjoys cooking for others, watch carefully, as he may eat little to nothing. Or, your partner may say that he's too rushed for breakfast or too tired for dinner. Since some people seem married to their jobs, this response to not eating may sound normal in today's world. However, abstinence from food can lead to exhaustion and depression—or even an escalation of mania.

ASK THE DOCTOR

What's a good diet for my bipolar partner?

Always check with a professional, but some sources indicate that a high-protein diet featuring fish with fatty acids and lots of leafy green vegetables helps to foster a healthy balance of chemicals in the brain. Also, a minimal amount of sugar (even limiting the intake of fresh fruit) can be beneficial.

Since everyone needs sustenance to survive, you need to make sure your partner has regular daily meals. Set aside time for breakfast and dinner—or even lunch if you're both at home. Try to avoid high-pressure or emergency situations that distract your partner from eating. Ideally, you'll eat balanced meals together, but if an emergency arises, grab a bag of snacks or anything for nourishment until you can sit your partner down for a regular meal.

Equally important is sufficient amounts of rest. People who work nights tend to get less sleep than people who work days because more activities are available during daytime hours. Therefore, if at all possible your partner should avoid working the night shift. If your partner works at home—and sometimes all night—remind him of your need to go to bed together. If your partner is a "TV-holic," set the timer on the television set and remind your partner that you need sufficient sleep to function the next day. A hot bath may help induce sleep, and herbal tea is another option. Other behaviors that can aid in falling asleep include the reading of a book before bedtime or listening to music. Your bedroom should also be dark and cool and, if possible, remove the clock from view. If your partner suffers from chronic insomnia, this information should be conveyed to the doctor.

Too Much Eating and Sleeping

Overeating, or binging, is a common practice for someone who is depressed. Mania can cause also cause people to overeat. For example, your partner might be a compulsive cook or become obsessed with determining the best topping for pizza or the best way to season a steak. If your partner is prone to compulsive eating, avoid "all you can eat" restaurants and avoid filling your cupboards with junk food. If your partner's overeating is symptomatic of depression, try to engage your partner in conversation so she can discuss what's on her mind. If she won't open up to you, you may want to contact her doctor. If it is obvious that your partner is not starving to death, don't be an enabler. If you run out of potato chips, don't purchase more. If your partner asks for more cookies, do not indulge her request. Junk food is not a substitute for nutrition.

Depression, as opposed to mania, frequently causes someone to sleep too much. Depressed people often take to their bed as a means to hide from the world, sometimes with empty bags of junk food. If your partner oversleeps from depression, contact the doctor; this information is important to convey. Try to offer short, safe steps outside of the bedroom or off of the sofa. If you have a yard area or a nearby park, encourage your partner to join you for a few moments outdoors. Or, offer to watch a movie together. At least your partner will be awake and connecting to another human being.

Excessive amounts of sleep can also be the end result of a manic phase, causing the person to collapse from exhaustion. In this case, it may be best to let your partner sleep it off. Components of behavioral activation therapy (discussed in Chapter 3) may help to address this issue.

Daily Hygiene

Poor sleeping habits may be the result of some obsession or compulsion to complete a particular project. Ultimately, this could be self-destructive. Insufficient sleep may also cause people to become too wired to care. For these bipolar patients, bothering to bathe, comb their hair, brush their teeth, shave, or put on clean clothes is unimportant. Sometimes they might even emit a pungent odor. Although certain medications may cause excessive perspiration, it may also be the result of poor hygiene and unclean clothing. Even though most adults do not like being told what to do, especially when pertaining to bodily hygiene, you can be frank with your partner by emphasizing how you are impacted by his odor or bad breath.

On the other hand, if your partner is spending endless hours curled up in bed, he may also be taking long baths or showers. While this can be therapeutic, long hours in the bathtub can also mean that he is seeking a womblike escape from the world, a variation of sleeping fourteen to sixteen hours a day. Medication therapy may help, but you and your partner's therapist might also encourage him to identify some small activity or accomplishment as a motivator to help overcome his paralyzing inertia. A major challenge of depression is the ability to transcend the current mind-body state by remembering and/or imagining a more satisfying and hopeful way of investing in life.

By recognizing the warning signals and being attentive to situations that may add fuel to your partner's symptoms, you remain in a better position to help your partner remain stable and avoid relapse. In Part II, we'll combine this knowledge with a focus on key concerns for maintaining a loving and fulfilling relationship and the impact of bipolar disorder in meeting this challenge.

PART II

BUILDING BLOCKS OF A RELATIONSHIP

While a loving relationship can survive in many forms, it requires certain elements for it to truly flourish and be fulfilling. Good communication, trust, and physical intimacy are three of these basic building blocks. By being mindful of these concerns, couples are helped to experience a true partnership that fosters openness, dependability, and a deepened commitment to the relationship. Your shared capacity to embrace these elements can be especially challenged when your partner has bipolar disorder. Part II offers a variety of approaches you can take to meet these challenges.

Chapter 6
Is Good Communication Possible?

Almost every expert on relationships advocates good communication as an essential ingredient for a rewarding and lasting relationship. It is through such communication that couples can attain a genuine understanding of each other and define both individual and shared goals. The capacity to freely and honestly share one's thoughts and feelings with a loved one reflects a deep level of trust and intimacy that is the foundation for a lasting commitment. But what exactly is "good communication"? And, more significantly, what challenges may you experience while trying to foster good communication with your partner who has bipolar disorder?

All Relationships Have Communication Issues

Almost everyone at some time finds it difficult to speak with another person. Such difficulty goes beyond asking your boss for a raise or confronting your overbearing mother-in-law. Sometimes it can seem like an act of courage just to ask your partner to turn the volume down on the television. Not because your relationship is abusive, but because the unspoken dynamics of your bond emerge between you and your partner over time: "Will I sound like a nag if I bring this up again?" or "Will I hurt his feelings if I tell him I don't eat veal?" At times, even thinking of expressing the smallest concern may lead to anxiety.

You may also believe that, in some way, you are the caretaker in your relationship and your needs are less relevant. You may view your bipolar partner as someone you need to nurture but who is not available to meet your needs. Perhaps you're driven by some underlying discomfort with being nurtured based on not wanting to feel weak and in need of support. Your role as caretaker may also derive from a genuine fear that you won't be able to depend on your partner to be there for you if and when you need him.

Without full awareness, your communication difficulties may stem from your need to maintain negative feelings toward your partner. This may be the case if, for example, over time you resent the sacrifices you make or if, by overlooking your own needs, you increasingly feel isolated and alone in your relationship. Harboring negative feelings toward your partner may serve as a distraction from the real disappointments that you experience in the relationship. In the extreme, you may start to believe your partner is a bad person and, by confirming this belief, you don't need to work at making things better. Although unaware of any subconscious desire, the subliminal need to maintain resentment may actually facilitate the task of ending a bad relationship.

Communicating Anger

In any relationship, it is often challenging to know when to say what without making a bad situation worse. This can be especially true in a bipolar relationship. Emotions can greatly override how we interpret what we hear. Perhaps you'll be greeted with a favorable response, but other times your comment may cause negative emotions in your partner, creating tension for both of you. At times, you may have hindsight about how you contributed to your partner's reaction. On other occasions you may have no clue as to how your comments could have had such a negative impact. Since nobody is perfect, we are all guilty at one time or another of saying something that our partner may not respond to as we might have hoped.

Part of the challenge in communicating is based on the fact that maintaining a healthy relationship involves some degree of compromise in order to preserve each partner's individual identity. It's reasonable that two individuals will need to address and share their unique perspectives and expectations as they work on their relationship. Because bipolar illness can involve impairment in judgment and emotion, what you say may not be heard as you intended and can subsequently arouse tension for both of you. As in any relationship, an occasional argument is normal—and actually improves communication—since it would be unrealistic to expect persons living together never to be in conflict. However, if arguments are frequent and pervasive you may need to consider couples counseling as a way of developing techniques to help you better communicate.

The discomfort many people experience with any form of anger is another factor that undermines candid communication, and the stress of coping with bipolar disorder can make both of you especially sensitive to this complex and challenging emotion. Too often people associate anger with rage or aggression. Rage can be scary for other people to witness, as the raging person seems out of control and unpredictable. It may be especially difficult for your bipolar partner to observe you in such a state and just as difficult for you if your partner appears to be enraged. Even when no one is physically injured, the sheer force of the rage can deeply wound the souls of those exposed to it. Nearly all anger is the reaction to other negative emotions, such as anxiety, shame, disappointment, frustration, or the feeling of being devalued or rejected. An honest relationship requires partners to directly communicate feelings of anger with each other. Direct communication of anger means sharing the feelings that lead to anger as well as the anger itself. It means talking about the anger and not "showing" it in angry behavior. You would, for example, be candid and direct by saying, "I am disappointed and become anxious when you do not take your medication. That makes me irritated."

CASE STUDY: Mike and Pat

Effective communication often requires patient self-reflection in order to identify what it is that you want to express. Mike, a forty-two-year-old married man, sought counseling at the request of his wife because of his increasing episodes of anger, which had escalated during the past several months. While Mike had a history of periodic verbal outbursts, he was becoming abusive in his language and, on several occasions, frightened his wife, Pat, a woman with a history of bipolar illness.

Mike initially focused much of his anger on his wife for a variety of issues that often related to the symptoms of her illness. In therapy, he learned to identify the negative emotions that fueled his anger when Pat hadn't behaved as he believed she "should." While initially only able to recognize his anger, he soon was able to acknowledge disappointment, frustration, a sense of inadequacy, and feelings of being powerless to impact his wife. Mike also admitted to personal disappointment and frustration for his inability to be more effective in helping Pat. Additionally, he experienced some levels of shame that accompanied his perceived failures.

Much of Mike's anger was related to his expectations regarding Pat's behavior and his ability to influence it. To address this, he was helped to clarify the ways he could control the situation and also when he could not impact change. At the same time, Mike became mindful of how he had personalized Pat's behaviors. On many occasions, when she was distracted by her symptoms, Mike was quick to conclude that Pat did not care for him or respect him. Instead, he learned to expect and accept that there would be times when Pat might not be fully present and considerate of him. Most significantly, he learned to be cognizant that his intense anger was, in reality, a revisiting of long-held feelings of not being cared for, which he had experienced years before his marriage. Through this realization, he was able better clarify what was important to communicate to Pat so she could more readily understand him when she was ready to listen.

"Good" communication requires hard work and never comes easy. It may even involve venturing into the unpleasant and difficult; but, it does not require excessive, annoying, or constantly probing communication. If you say, "I think I'll get a glass of water," and your partner says, "What do you mean by that?" your partner needs to lighten up. Good communication entails a shared sense of humor, mutual and good-natured teasing, and sometimes just a few words of encouragement.

In a relationship with a bipolar person, it might be useful to remember that no relationship has "perfect" communication and that many of the challenges you face are the same as in any loving relationship. Still, some challenges to effective communication are unique to a relationship when one of the partners has bipolar disorder.

The Elephant in the Room

The fact that your partner has bipolar disorder can never be fully ignored in regard to its potential impact on your communication. If your partner has an excellent response to treatment, it may have little if any effect on the communication in the relationship even though your awareness of the illness may play a role in how and when you bring up certain issues. However, if treatment is only partially successful, or if your partner is not on medication therapy or in the middle of a manic or depressive episode, then complications may emerge to confound the communication process.

Will My Partner Have an Episode?

Even if your partner appears stable in his moods, you may be afraid that bringing something up will trigger an episode. You may fear that any news, even good news, may trigger mania. Conversely, you may fear that bad news will lead to serious depression. Beyond a certain point you must let life unfold, and your partner has the right to know the facts. If you are still concerned about the potential response to what you need to communicate, seek a professional for advice or to be present when you confront your partner. If the issue is less serious, go ahead and tell your partner that you wrecked the car, got a huge raise, that she hogs all the blankets at night, or whatever it is you want to say.

Will My Partner Be Too Out-of-It to Care?

At the other extreme, your partner's medication regime may tend to make him feel flattened out emotionally and unable to react to your news. Sometimes the need for medicating symptoms is so great that the bipolar patient cannot do anything other than stay home and watch television. Even if he holds down a job he may seem out of touch or unable to remember what you tell him.

For example, let's say you just found out something tragic: your brother was in a car accident and is in serious condition. You really want your partner to be there for you—to listen, to hold you, to bring you real comfort. While your bipolar partner may usually be able to do all this, the impact of his medication may make him unavailable to provide you any emotional support. He may even seem hurtful at such moments. You state that your brother is in the hospital, and your partner replies, "Gee, that's too bad. I'm sorry to hear it. What should we have for dinner?"

WORD TO THE WISE

Do Unto Others

You know how challenging it can be when someone wants to initiate a conversation when you are transitioning from one activity to another. Such moments may even be more difficult for your partner. For example, when you walk in the door following a full day's work, you may prefer time out to get settled before being confronted with your partner's wish to discuss vacation plans. Nevertheless, your bipolar partner deserves equal consideration.

At such moments, you need to remember that the illness, perhaps in combination with the side effects of the medication, undermines his capacity to be fully present and positively responsive. It may be useful to drop a small hint, or be very specific, to assist your partner in focusing his attention. This may push you beyond your comfort level, but it may be necessary to directly ask: "Would you please hold me for a while?"

Will My Partner Be Too Self-Absorbed to Care?

When medication is only partially effective, or if your significant other isn't on medication, there may be moments of mania and depression that compete with your need to communicate. If your partner is manic, she may seem extremely agitated, as if she just drank ten espressos in a row. She may not sit still or may speak so quickly and so forcefully that you're unable to reply. In this frame of mind, she may think nothing of interrupting you in midsentence and changing the topic. This incomprehensible monologue goes nowhere and everywhere simultaneously. Moreover, in this frame of mind your partner may seem to have little regard for your feelings and be extremely blunt and hurtful without even knowing it.

For example, after speaking with your sister on the telephone, you may report to your partner, "I feel terrible. Cathy and Brian are getting divorced." Your partner replies, and does it so rapidly that you can barely comprehend let alone interject, "Well, I saw it coming. Didn't you? They really weren't right for each other. I know they went to counseling, but I didn't think that could fix it. Speaking of fixing, I've been trying and trying to get someone over here to look at the leaky faucet. I got seven estimates today, but none of them were any good. I've been thinking anyway, maybe we should just remodel the kitchen. I saw some great ideas in the magazine." And so on.

CASE STUDY: Ann and Mark

Ann and her husband Mark were collaborating on a children's book, but Mark frequently needed to remind Ann to slow down, take a break, and refocus. He states, "She writes for hours without coming up for air. Then, she wants my undivided attention, but it's always on her timetable. She will complete a chapter and present it to me as a 'fait accompli,' and I sometimes find myself pulling away. I know that these signs are symptoms of Ann's bipolar condition, but it's difficult to deal with her when she's so off-balance. She expects me to drop everything and listen, and her fixation is reflected both in her tone and rate of speech as if something big is about to happen. There's an aura of excitement about her, but as we sit for long periods I feel disjointed, somehow distant, like I'm viewing a special effects scene at a movie theater. I'm drawn into the drama, yet not fully a part." During periods of self-reflection, Ann admits that Mark seems edgy when she confronts him on these occasions. Mark's response: "She rambles on and on, which leaves me with a twinge of sadness. I find myself asking, Is it me? Or, is it something about Ann?"

In time, Mark began to grow weary of Ann's apparent highs and lows and, likewise, she became increasingly disenchanted by what she considered to be Mark's insensitivity to her affliction. The dilemma so exacerbated Ann's distress that her self-confidence eroded to a temporary new low.

When Ann and Mark reached the final editing stages of the book, their work pace quickened. She telephoned Mark at his office more regularly during this period, and he felt her calls were all about "trivial details unrelated to the book." Ann says, "Mark complained that my messages carried a sense of urgency and that my points were sometimes repetitive. When Mark did not immediately pick up the call, I left messages. I am accustomed to replying quickly to telephone messages, faxes, and e-mail correspondence. Mark, on the other hand, does not. He gives himself what he considers 'a comfortable window for response,' which works for him but annoys me. It seemed clear that Mark and I had different ideas about what is 'important.' My manner of dealing was to wait an hour or two and if he didn't call or e-mail back, I sometimes repeated the message if I felt it was important and could not wait. Is it possible, I thought, that heightened tension has prompted

Mark to hold the relationship with me at bay by keeping it narrowly defined? He had apparently begun to distance himself.

"Finally, Mark attempted to structure our conversations about the book so they did not exceed ten to fifteen minutes. I found this restriction exasperating. 'What's your goal, Ann?' Mark would ask. Frequent clashes resulted because it is difficult and unnatural for me to talk 'bottom line.' I envisioned an imaginary time clock, and in order to get in all my thoughts I began to talk faster and faster."

Several months after Mark and Ann had completed working on their book, he described his thoughts in a short personal essay: "Ann is speaking louder and faster. Her voice is strident, the sweetness gone. How does she have time to breathe between words? She accuses me of being critical of her. I feel I am not being heard. In frustration, I put down the phone and walk away. When I return a few minutes later, Ann is still talking; she did not even notice my absence.

It's Tuesday afternoon and my answering machine is blinking to be played. My e-mail box is full with messages sent by Ann. I let out a sigh and ignore them. Many times there is no new information. Or I receive six e-mails all the same, each addressed to a different recipient on which I am copied."

Over a period of months, Ann and Mark's relationship eroded further and they kept each other at a comfortable distance. Ann worried about their marriage ending since the tension between them had heightened. Mark was setting limits and beginning to apply the brakes. In looking back, Ann can now see how Mark's frustration over this matter must have heated up to the point of actual boiling. But she, too, was at the brink of explosion. Both are strong-willed individuals with different priorities and working styles that just didn't mesh. What kept them together was the strength of their bond and a mutual desire to work through their problems.

When you care about your bipolar partner, it's possible to see the light side of her personality while being accepting of her quirkiness. Nevertheless, it can be exasperating in the moment, especially if you are unaccustomed to this kind of reaction. At such times, try to remember that it's the mania—the illness—talking. Be prepared to bring up whatever you have said again because your manic partner is likely to forget what you said. You may even consider putting off addressing the subject until things calm down. But if things do not settle down soon, or if what you need to communicate cannot wait, try to re-create the scene to emphasize the importance of what you want to say. Keep the conversation brief.

For example, you may try to make your partner think that listening to you is his ultimate task of the moment: "I have to ask a favor. I need to say something very important because I trust you, and I need you to sit down with me and listen." Physical contact, such as clasping hands, maintaining eye contact, and speaking slowly in a modulated tone of voice may also help to emphasize the urgency of your message. Since your partner is in a very active mode, he may welcome the chance to do something for you. Next, you might add: "I only have a few minutes to talk, so I need to just say it." Wait briefly for a response. Based on your partner's reaction, you may decide to continue speaking or just thank him for listening and end the conversation.

If your partner is feeling depressed, he may not welcome your conversation and may instead appear moody and disinterested. If you think you can snap him out of his depression by sharing bad news of your own, you should reconsider. His depression stems from a serious illness and cannot be diffused by subtle strategies.

Nor will small talk aimed at changing the subject distract him from his own unhappiness.

What may seem evident needs emphasizing: nobody enjoys being depressed. If a depressed person could merely "snap out of it," he would. This may be especially difficult to remember when you unrealistically expect that your partner will be more fully present with you. Understandably, you may be prone to frustration when he refuses to go to a movie or follow through with a simple house chore or must be coaxed to get out of bed.

Hopefully, a professional is monitoring your partner's depression so, for now, keep communication with your loved as straightforward as possible. Some things will need to be shared, and you should, by all means, listen to your partner if she wants to talk about the depression with you. You may even want to gently approach the subject yourself, and remind her how much you care. Without a gentle reminder, she may erroneously conclude that you are angry, don't want to discuss the issue, or have given up on her. Whatever the situation, it is the wrong time to expect any kind of mutual give and take. When your partner's depression becomes severe, you may question her feelings toward you—did she ever did care? Do what you can to help, talk to your loved one's doctor, and re-evaluate the situation when the depression lifts. What appeared to be disinterest was likely a symptom of the depression that took away all sense of your partner's joy. Once she feels better, her love for you may well be intact.

Don't Forget Your Own Needs

When your partner is manic or depressed, it's probably not the best time to sit down and discuss the state of your relationship, but what if it seems like there's never a good time? Is it just the bipolar disorder or are there other factors involved?

Some people naturally shy away from revealing too much information about themselves, especially concerning their relationships.

Others chatter incessantly but talk about nothing deep or serious. They may feel uncomfortable and self-conscious or may not be fully in touch with their feelings. Others may harbor fears and insecurities unrelated to their bipolar condition. Perhaps, for example, your partner comes from a family that demonstrated very little love and acceptance, or where the children were denied the ability to express how they felt. Consider your partner's background. What are her family members like? Do her siblings also complain about personal problems, even though they are not bipolar? Do you also dislike her parents?

ASK THE DOCTOR

Does everyone get depressed?

Rare is the person who never feels depressed and, since emotions are contagious, you may find yourself experiencing some level of depression along with your partner. If the condition persists, seek professional help. However, your own experience may help you respond to your bipolar partner. If you find yourself losing patience, try remembering a time when you felt low. Did you feel hopeless, as though nothing could ever make you feel good again? Empathy is important to all relationships.

Always remember that people—bipolar or not—may have many reasons for not being good communicators. If their condition is unrelated to bipolar disorder, you may decide that something needs to be done. With the guidance of a professional, you may explain to your partner that you feel the two of you never really talk and that you want to correct this because you want to feel closer to him. If the bipolar symptoms seem responsible for the communication difficulties, in part because of treatment, express these concerns in a professional setting, as well.

Should little change over time, even with the help of a professional, you may want to explore your options. Some people grow to accept that their partner is not a good communicator but feel that the relationship is still satisfying. Others begin to feel lonelier than before they became a couple. If you have tried every avenue and your needs are not being met, consider your alternatives.

When It's Hard to Talk to Your Partner

We have identified many scenarios in which bipolar disorder, its treatment, and related factors can limit communication. In the following discussion, we highlight several patterns of reaction that you may fall into when dealing with communication difficulties. We encourage you to be mindful of falling into such patterns and offer strategies to avoid the pitfalls.

The Fake Happy Person

You may find yourself unwittingly gravitating toward fake happiness when your partner is depressed. Without full awareness, couples often embark on a division of labor for all aspects of their life. Simply put, if one of you is unhappy, the other might feel compelled to act happy in order to balance things out. However, happiness may be difficult when the person you love is sad. You're probably worried about what comes next: Will this all-pervasive gloom never end? Will he need hospitalization? Will there be a suicide attempt?

Due to these worries, the "happiness" you display probably feels insincere. In fact, your facade of happiness may be unsettling to you and to others because its lack of authenticity creates tension. Your partner may also feel it. Depressed as he is, your partner may inform you in rather harsh terms how he feels about your "mask" of happiness. While you're trying to remind your partner that life holds goodness and beauty, your timing is off since you're neither seeing nor feeling what you profess as fact. No matter how good your intensions, nobody likes a phony.

Be mindful of maintaining realistic expectations while remaining determined to survive your partner's depression. Also, do whatever possible to make sure he is getting the best professional help possible. Simultaneously, seek out support groups for yourself or confide in people whom you trust to respect your feelings. Allow yourself to be sad or cheerful as the mood strikes you, and remember that nobody benefits from a lack of authenticity.

WORD TO THE WISE

It's Okay to Cry

If your partner wants to cry, even seemingly about nothing, let it happen. You may even find yourself in tears. Crying is an emotional release, but additional counseling for your partner may be justified if she is sobbing uncontrollably.

The Pipsqueak

When your partner is manic and barely lets you interject a word while busying himself with matters of no concern to you or, perhaps, involves you against your wishes, you may feel like a pipsqueak—something small and insignificant, yet annoying. In reaction to your partner's overwhelming (and at times overbearing) emotionality, you may experience a kind of age regression where you feel like the only child in a roomful of grownups. This experience may lead you to tap into the kind of loneliness or frustrating sense of insignificance that you may have felt as a child. As that child of your youth, you maybe felt paralyzed to speak up and protect yourself, so you found passive-aggressive ways of making your displeasure known. Today, you may act moody, hoping that someone asks what is wrong, but no one does. Even if someone does inquire, you make the fatal error of answering "nothing," rather than availing yourself of the opportunity for some honest communication. But, given the way you feel, you cannot speak up.

If you're in this state of mind, it may be best to go off in your own direction to regain your full adult sense of self. However, you may feel the need to remain close by in case the situation gets out of hand or you may not be able to bring yourself to disengage. In such a state, you may experience a sense of paralysis, feeling you deserve to be belittled and ignored, so you passively react to your discomfort. For example, you may tag along with your manic partner while she goes on a shopping spree while never asking if there is anything you want to look at or purchase. Perhaps you think you have a better chance of keeping expenses down by being there—and maybe you can—but be careful that you don't get yourself into trouble by going along with your partner's impaired, manic judgment.

Although you may be steaming in silent resentment, vowing never to accompany your partner again or perhaps considering a break-up—anything other than accompanying your partner in the moment—stay put! Sharing your dissatisfaction in a compassionate manner will be better for both of you.

The Copycat

While partners sometimes seek to balance each other, at other times they want to copy each other. It is not unusual for people in a relationship to acquire a taste for a food or style of music enjoyed by their partner. Perhaps her hobby now becomes your hobby, or his favorite vacation place is now your favorite. The propensity to adopt the likes and dislikes of a partner is a natural reaction of being in a close relationship, much the same as children who discover new ways from parents or friends.

Even if you disagree politically or maintain different religious beliefs, over time you'll probably empathize with your partner's point of view. Sometimes things go a step further, and one party converts to the other's religion or political party. Perhaps you never got angry about environmental issues until your partner instilled you with anger. Or, you take your partner's side in a dispute with a third party even though that might not have happened had you been single.

Many partners adopt each other's moods and feelings, but this phenomenon takes on a special meaning in a relationship with a bipolar person. Although you cannot become bipolar, you may innocently get into the manic or depressed mood of the moment. For example, if your partner is depressed and moping about the house, or sleeping or eating too much or too little, you may feel compelled to imitate his behavior: if he's not hungry, neither are you; he feels tired, so do you; he doesn't want to venture out, so neither do you. You agree that life stinks. If your partner is manic, you are having the best time in the world in his company. You laugh, go places, and do things. You may even join your partner in binge drinking or overspending.

At such moments, mirroring your partner may derive from your wish to feel closer and more united. Again, you cannot will yourself to be bipolar, but perhaps you can empathize or identify with your partner's extreme high or devastating low. In this situation your strength in empathizing has led to "empathy gone awry" and you may now be unable to step back and view your partner objectively.

These are not wise behavioral choices to make. Mania and depression harm the self on many levels, and your own lighter, semi-genuine versions of these feelings can cause you personal harm. Take good care of yourself, and remember that entering into a world of unwise choices is unhealthy and can be dangerous.

Good communication helps foster trust in a relationship, and building and maintaining trust is the prerequisite to promoting honesty and directness in communication. In the following chapter, we will highlight those factors that deserve attention in establishing a relationship based on trust with your bipolar partner.

Chapter 7
Is Trust Possible?

When we enter any relationship we bring with us a personal history that informs and influences our expectations of trust in that relationship. Hopefully, as our new relationship unfolds we develop a growing trust, one based on an increased sense of an emotional alliance and dependability. Yet, there are times when a partner may disappoint us, based either on our own misperceptions or by genuinely not living up to our expectations. So, what about someone who has a mental condition that may compel him to do things he may not normally do? Can you trust your bipolar partner? For that matter, can he trust you, given that you may have to report his behavior if it grows extreme? The fact that bipolar people sometimes suffer paranoid delusions may also undermine your partner's trust in you. While issues regarding trust are a part of every relationship, loving someone with bipolar illness brings with it unique concerns for both establishing and maintaining trust.

All Relationships Have Trust Issues

No one ever fully knows another person. Even couples married for fifty years have things they have never told each other. And it is not necessarily because they are ashamed or deceitful. It can simply be because the human memory is faulty or that we sometimes have a very biased version of events. It can also be because we simply don't think something is worth mentioning or that mentioning it will lead to unnecessary complications.

ASK THE DOCTOR

How important is honesty?

If you feel that communication between you and your partner is not good, you may want to consider how much and how well you communicate rather than placing the blame entirely on the other person. In general, bipolar people love to talk, so what you may need is more experience or training in helping to guide the conversation in meaningful ways.

Sharing personal information about ourselves or keeping secrets is one of the major ways we determine what type of relationship we will have with other people. It is a way to measure or express how much we care about them. We want Person A to know something but not Person B, because we like and trust Person A more. There would be no coupling or best friendships if we could not make our own choices about how much to share with whom. Besides, we need to know that our lives and the decisions we make, for better or worse, ultimately belong to us and not somebody else. What to share and with whom are our choices to make. Additionally, the capacity to not have to share everything reflects an ability to comfortably live within one's own skin. It reflects to some degree a healthy relationship with oneself that does not always need an audience, validation, or advice regarding daily decisions and challenges.

Even when we do share something, we keep in mind how much to share and how to share such information; how you describe an incident to your best friend may be different from how you describe it to your mother-in-law. We also talk about our version of events. Sometimes we're willing to admit we're wrong or that whatever happened was at least partially our fault—particularly, when the topic in question happened some time ago. But most of the time, when we talk about ourselves and what we've done, we tend to make ourselves out to be the "good guy." Many people have a difficult time admitting personal faults and often attempt to "save face" regarding how others perceive them—and how they perceive themselves.

Imperfect beings that we are, sometimes we do things that we want to conceal from our partners. Sometimes decent and honest people fib to their partner about when they paid a bill, how the car got dented, or whether they gave Junior a candy bar when he was not supposed to have one. Whereas we might appear accepting and forgiving of such minor transgressions, these little "white lies" may help us preserve our sense of self—an identity more comfortable to live with than that exposed under full disclosure.

You may draw some comfort in acknowledging that "mini" secrets are common to all relationships and that loving someone bipolar is not unique in this respect. Trust issues have little to do with the fact that you have a bipolar partner, but if his symptoms are amplifying, other considerations should be kept in mind.

Learn to Recognize Acting-Out

Let's revisit the major bipolar symptoms: on a basic level, is your partner seeming to lapse into depression and/or mania? Does he seem indifferent? Is it impossible for her to sit still? Is he eating and sleeping? Does she not want to talk? Is he speaking nonstop and very rapidly? Remember that these sudden behavioral changes may signal an impending episode. These behaviors may similarly suggest that your partner is experiencing some form of stress that has triggered her symptoms. Be mindful that she may be concealing alcohol abuse, her negligence in following a medication regimen, or even an insufficient sleep pattern. If any of these signals are apparent, start looking deeper. At such moments it may be helpful to trust your distrust rather than ignore or minimize it.

Money Issues

Seemingly out of nowhere, a person can make unwise investments or business decisions during a manic phase. He may elect to buy everyone in the bar an expensive bottle of champagne or impulsively fly out of town to go gambling. Your partner may even decide to give a large sum of money to a best friend, a relative, or to some worthy cause. Since mania involves an inflated sense of self, it can naturally lead to compulsive spending.

WORD TO THE WISE

Avoid the Use of Money as Medication

Many people take pleasure in the "plastic cure" when unhappy or worried, as if the ability to charge anything they want—even if unaffordable—will make them feel better. They don't realize their high is temporary and will end abruptly with their next credit card bill.

The high that comes with compulsive spending is similar to what an alcoholic feels when she reaches for a bottle. The person who feels invisible may reach for the credit card as a way to convince herself that she deserves whatever she can get and no one should stand in her way. Spending can be a self-soothing strategy, an approach that confirms the feeling of being at least "okay," if not better than others. That part of the self that would normally say "slow down, you're wrecking your life" is not functioning during a manic attack.

At other times your partner may not spend money but will create other emotional challenges by how he manages money. For example, he may feel paranoid enough to withdraw all your shared savings to keep the money "safe" at home. Deceit regarding money undermines trust and, in the extreme, conflicts over money can end a relationship. Adults want to feel a sense of financial autonomy. To be denied access to household resources is humiliating and can make an adult feel as though he's being treated like a child. The resulting feeling of inequality is a motivating force for a bipolar partner to keep secrets from his mate.

Monitoring Money

If you know your partner has a history of spending problems and her symptoms are out of control, you may need to understand the details of her binging to maintain a trusting relationship.

For starters, try monitoring your account balances online. If some accounts are more difficult to access, consider converting them to a more accessible and secure venue. If your partner is manic and some of your money is unaccounted for, you need to set boundaries.

If your partner has a history of money issues driven by mania, work out a system to minimize a reoccurrence. Perhaps you want a joint account but also private accounts for both you and your partner so you can save or spend as you choose. The joint account (or investments) can be set up to require both signatures. You can also speak confidentially with a banker or an accountant about additional strategies. If your partner still finds a way around these security measures, it may be time for tough love and a new approach so the only money your partner receives is what you give her. Should your partner complain, be firm. Explain that if the relationship is to continue, the plan is not negotiable. You may want to find other things that your partner can take responsibility for, like landscaping the yard or selecting a new refrigerator, while you handle the finances. Although this approach may at times feel uncomfortable, know that you are protecting both of you from a potentially damaging outcome.

If you are engaged in a serious conversation—possibly in a professional setting—money issues should be part of that discussion. Some people neglect to discuss money, especially in a conversation of some depth, but if you are hurt, angry, and frustrated when the budget falls apart, you can—and should—express those thoughts. You may even mention your sadness, anxiety, and disappointment when compulsive overspending diminishes your shared potential to enjoy a more rewarding life. More importantly, your partner's impulsive choices can create financial debt that both of you may carry for many years. Most significant, you need to underscore how binge spending undermines your trust in your partner and your relationship.

Work Issues

While some bipolar sufferers can successfully hold a job, others cannot. Even if highly successful, there may be periods where your partner is unable to work because of his bipolar symptoms. If you're not independently wealthy, this sudden departure from work can be a significant, long-term loss of household income.

This also means your partner will be spending more time at home. Although this can be nice, it can potentially lead to further conflict and problems. When there is less order in your partner's life, he may fill the void with unconstructive activities. Any lack of structure coupled with mania can lead to extra purchases that could add to your financial difficulties.

Frequently, someone who is unemployed for a period of time begins to enjoy her idle status. After being discouraged by repeated rejections when seeking new employment, people prone to depression are likely to feel that they need a few days, a week, or even a month to recover from their disappointment. At such moments, your partner may conclude that she has not made progress, or that her disorder will prevent her from succeeding in the future. This is a time when your love and affection is most needed, and a little TLC can go a long way. Your partner may also benefit from talking to an employment counselor about how to handle job interviews. It's beneficial to schedule this appointment as soon as possible—even the same day—since mania can lead to very unfocused behavior and a million other things might stand in the way of your partner keeping a scheduled appointment. With a little humor, you can encourage your partner to seek help now rather than later—other things can wait, and "later" can be never.

WORD TO THE WISE

Create an Advanced Directive

One of the most important things you can do in a bipolar relationship is to create an advance directive. This is a signed legal document in which your bipolar partner gives permission for another individual (such as a doctor or family member) to ensure that she receives proper treatment—even hospitalization—should she experience another episode.

At the same time, let her know that your trust depends more on what she does to help herself and the relationship than on whether she maintains a specific job.

Violent Impulses

During severe manic episodes, a bipolar individual may become very harmful to himself or others. This may involve violence up to and including murder or suicide. If a manic person feels seriously threatened, there may be an eruption of violent behavior. By contrast, the desire to escape the intense anxiety and agitation that may accompany these episodes is often a major aspect of the motivation for suicide.

Even if murder or suicide is not the outcome, a bipolar person can seriously harm herself through reckless mania or a botched suicide attempt. Likewise, she can bring injury to others by causing a serious accident or expressing anger through physical violence. It's understandable that the unpredictability of behavior during such episodes may greatly undermine your capacity to trust your partner.

If your partner gets violent, you should leave immediately. Don't assume you can calm your partner down. If you must sneak out or make up some excuse to leave, do whatever is necessary to stay safe. If you have children, take them with you. If you have a cell phone, enter 911 and the local police department number into your speed dial. You may also want to put a close friend or a family member on speed dial. Ideally, this should be someone who can manage an emergency. Remember, no one deserves an abusive relationship, and physical assault of another person is against the law. Unfortunately, there is no guarantee that the violence will stop.

Can I Believe What My Partner Says?

Even in less dramatic scenarios, your manic partner may demonstrate behaviors that make you wonder how much you can trust her. She may, for example, burst into a talking marathon chatting about anything and everything. Sometimes the chatter digresses into rhyming or stoned-like incoherence, but even before this happens you may wonder if your partner is being truthful or just talking to talk. This can mean that your partner is telling possible untruths about actual situations, opinions, and attitudes. For example, she is a Democrat, but she gets into a long-drawn-out discussion with a Republican and suddenly claims to be Republican. Depression can compel people to say many things they would never say if not depressed: "Life is hopeless," "Nobody cares about me," and so on.

WORD TO THE WISE
No Guns Allowed

If your bipolar partner is interested in guns or other weapons, even for display purposes, it's wise to insist he take up a different hobby. Be honest. Say that you worry about guns in the house and that he should do this for you.

Since manic behaviors may leave you disoriented and questioning what really is true, it may be wise to accept your partner's talking marathons with a grain of salt. Many of us exaggerate at times or agree just for the sake of agreeing, but depression distorts reality in a different way. When things are calm, your bipolar partner is not necessarily any more honest or dishonest than the next person.

Setting Adult Boundaries

Part of being an adult is accepting who you are and determining guidelines and structure for how you want to live your life. Simultaneously, a loving relationship requires realistic compromises based on trust and candid communication. You can always ask your partner if he wants to behave in a certain way that may be more consistent with your expectation of how a relationship should be. Similarly, he is free to decide and to compromise if he chooses to do so. However, you cannot will your partner's bipolar disorder away, nor can you control the effectiveness of his treatment. But, you can choose to accept these realities and work things out accordingly.

CASE STUDY: Rick and Susan

Conflicts surrounding control issues can surface in any relationship. And when they do occur, they can greatly impact the level of trust between partners. Certain dynamics in a bipolar relationship may make both of you vulnerable to having such conflicts. This is what transpired for Rick, age thirty-eight, and Susan, thirty-two.

Rick was diagnosed with bipolar disorder during the second year of their six-year relationship. This diagnosis immediately moved Susan into a familiar situation, as she had played a very active and involved role in caring for her mother, who had a history of depression. From early adolescence on, often to the neglect of her own needs, Susan devoted much of her time and concern with her mother. For this reason, she felt very prepared to focus all of her energies on helping Rick to manage his illness. However, although well intended, Susan's intense vigilance regarding Rick's well-being and her detailed attention to his behavior gradually left him feeling treated like a child. He brought to the relationship his own sensitivity to feeling controlled, as he had grown up with a mother who was overly intrusive and minimally respected his boundaries. This left him, at times, prone to self-doubt and, in part, more vulnerable to not feeling independent. Subsequently, Rick had a predisposition to perceive Susan as being more like a parent than a loving partner.

Rick's resentment increased in the two years following his diagnosis. Rather than discuss his reactions, he would become irritable and at times explosive. In an attempt to experience greater control over his life, he became increasingly less communicative and isolated himself. His withdrawal fostered Susan's anxiety and distrust, which only increased her desire to be vigilant.

While Susan acted from her deep love for her partner, she had unwittingly behaved in ways that actually left Rick feeling abandoned, desiring a loving partner, and feeling more like she was a parent. The dynamics of their interactions led to a breakdown in trust and much turmoil that impaired effective communications. It was only after Rick's repeated episodes of anger that he and Ann both sought counseling to help them understand how their interactions undermined their mutual trust.

Tough Love

If you want a teenager to think you are cool and a "best friend," you can sit back and let him have complete say about whether or not he attends school, uses drugs, or what time he returns home at night. Or, you can risk having him get angry with you—even temporarily hate you—by insisting he stay in school, telling him that he must have a curfew, and that under no circumstances is he to use drugs. Similarly, if your mate is starting to show signs of mania or depression, you can sit back and let it happen to avoid having conflict and anger directed toward you. Or, for the good of your partner and all concerned, you can take one or all of the following actions:

- ***Call the doctor.*** If your partner is seeing a doctor, call her and report that various symptoms seem to be acting up.
- ***Call a family member or friend.*** Let someone you trust know what is happening. If things get truly bad, you (and your children) should have a place you can go temporarily.
- ***Check around the house.*** No one likes to feel spied on, and people who snoop around usually feel guilty or afraid of getting caught. Still, carefully looking things over can be in the best interest of you and your partner. For example, are there unfamiliar folders about business ventures or vacations? Are

there unfamiliar names with telephone numbers? Are there objects that could be used to cause harm?

- *Check medication adherence.* Is your partner taking her medication? Taking too much medication? Has your partner introduced another medication or herbal supplement? These suggestions are not intended to make you overly anxious or hypervigilant, but rather to alert you to areas of concern.
- *Look for changes in routines.* If your partner works outside the home, has he been going to work? Has he shown changes in the time he goes to bed or wakes up? Has he abruptly stopped an exercise regimen that he has been following? Has there been a change in your partner's social contacts?
- *Talk to your partner.* Explain that some recent behaviors appear symptomatic of an episode. Make it clear that you're not passing judgment, but that you have noticed (for example) that she has not eaten in twenty-four hours and that you're concerned and want to accompany her to the doctor or do whatever it takes to help.

Learning from Mistakes

Since no relationship is perfect, frequently a couple's best approach is to learn from past mistakes. While some partners never get past the stage of mistrust, others manage to stay together. Re-establishing trust requires a shared acceptance that the problem is abating or has been eliminated.

Talk It Over

When your partner has calmed down, take this opportunity to talk about what happened in a nonconfrontational tone. When you have arrived at some understanding, you can mutually decide how things can be improved in the future. Couples counseling is recommended, but even if you're seeing a therapist the two of you need to make time to talk together.

ASK THE DOCTOR

How can I manage conflict?

One effective guideline to help couples manage conflict is to agree in advance on a key word that can be used as a signal to drop a contentious subject during a heated discussion. For example, choose whimsical words such as "cheese ball," "monkey," or "jelly bean." Either partner can use the key signal with the understanding that the issue will be discussed at a later time when you have both cooled off. While this tactic will not work if your partner is severely manic, it can be useful at other times.

One of your big surprises might be the discovery of how your partner feels. When one partner assumes responsibility for the stability of the relationship, there is the tendency to forget about the other person's needs and feelings. Helping someone does not guarantee their gratitude. Even with the best of intentions, your partner may feel resentful about her dependent role and inability to contribute. Eventually, the dependent partner will begin to feel infantilized. Feeling treated like a child leads to resentment and the need to act out, a way of regaining some sense of independence and "equal" adult status.

Keep in mind that people who seem to enjoy or to expect others to wait on them want to also have the choice of acting independently. While most of us enjoy occasional pampering, few are comfortable being overindulged. Do not assume that your partner should be shielded from all frustration because of his bipolar illness. While too much stress can be overwhelming, learning to effectively manage frustration fosters a sense of mastery and self-confidence.

Although you may, at times, distrust that your partner can manage frustration on her own, being in tune with her history will help you feel fortified and accepting of this challenge.

WORD TO THE WISE

Use Compassion

Remember, when your partner is acting out his illness, it's not intentional. Conversely, if you lose patience with your partner and purposefully make her feel badly, you're acting without compassion. When intentionally inflicting pain, you may be reacting from your own discomfort. Your hurt needs to be addressed, and you'll neither help yourself nor your relationship by causing your partner pain. Be aware of your motives when communicating with your partner.

It's essential that you're aware of these tendencies and that you and your partner discuss the challenges as they occur. Conversations of this nature may be difficult to begin, but if the issues are ignored your partner may start acting out her feelings rather than discussing them. Talking things out can lead to self-discovery for both of you. Your partner might find better ways of articulating what his symptoms feel like, and you can be more in touch with your own feelings and needs by expressing them.

Protection Can Mean Love

While being attentive to how you impact the relationship, there may be times when you need to change the name on an account, add or change the locks, or enforce new rules. By approaching delicate matters in a loving way, your partner won't feel like you are treating him like a child. You can convey your intentions of keeping everyone safe and happy by heeding the new regimen. Try to address these security concerns in a collaborative manner. For example, if your partner acknowledges that he is in agreement about his not having access to important documents, this allows you to begin a discussion of alternative strategies for their safekeeping.

You may also point out that you still feel loved and protected by your partner in many different ways. Besides protecting your finances, the trust you have in your partner may depend on him taking proper care of himself. Sometimes you may need to play an active role in ensuring that he does so. For example, firmly communicate that while you understand your partner is feeling angry or depressed, you will not listen to him until he has something to eat. You may even need to abide by a strictly observed bedtime. Any of these guidelines can be done in a manner that conveys genuine love and concern rather than a harsh tone that sounds like a demand for obedience.

Do Not Be a Scapegoat

Occasionally you may even blame yourself for your partner's behavior. For example, you may recall having supported his request for one more beer at a party when you might have prevented his indulgence. Or, maybe because of your desire to enjoy an evening with friends, you convinced your partner to stay out later than usual. If your partner tries to blame you for his resulting mania or depression, don't let yourself become a scapegoat and berate yourself with guilt. Remember, even if you did contribute to his mood change, it is his illness that makes him vulnerable. Learn from your actions and be more mindful in the future.

You may also be blamed for your partner's reactions even when you did nothing to trigger them. At such moments, always remember the true nature of bipolar disorder. If he accuses you of placing the responsibility on him for his own symptoms, let your partner know that the blame game is not the point. If there is any possibility that he might be right, apologize while reminding him that the goal is not to point fingers but rather figure out a solution. Always keep the tone on an adult level.

ASK THE DOCTOR

What are some positive aspects about living with a bipolar partner?

One potentially positive aspect of living with a bipolar person who acts out from time to time is to learn an important lesson about what to take personally and what to let go. This is especially true if you tend to have your own "trigger points" that make you sensitive to criticism. Though challenging, you need to remember that it is your partner's illness talking and go about your business, even if what was said about you was not nice.

Your partner may even be camouflaging her own sense of guilt and embarrassment by lashing out at you. This may not be fair, but it's about your partner's inability to cope; it is not about you. It might be comforting to remind yourself of this, while simultaneously reminding your partner that everyone messes up at times. Nobody is perfect. It is through such compassionate communication that you can experience a sense of alliance with each other and achieve mutual trust.

What Can You Do Differently?

Once the crisis has passed, take an inventory of yourself. Have you made mistakes? For example:

- **Did you yell at your kids, friends, or coworkers because of your frustration with your partner?** If so, apologize and deal with your own stress issues. Talk to a professional if you believe it will help.
- **Did you neglect your own needs and responsibilities?** Did you end up not eating or sleeping? Did you have to miss work?

- **Do you have unrealistic expectations for your partner, given the relative severity of his condition?** If your bipolar partner realistically cannot work outside the home, you need to decide if you can accept and live with this decision. By contrast, if you harbor completely unrealistic expectations of what you would like your partner to become, release them, because all they are doing is hurting you, your partner, and your relationship.
- **Do you still love your partner?** This is a tough one. You may feel guilty if the answer is "no," because you don't want to hurt him or you feel that he "needs" you. You may even feel it is a sign of weakness or selfishness on your part to value concerns like financial stability over caring for another person.

Remember, trust in any relationship involves being candid with each other whether the goal is to promote a growing relationship or to end one. While the latter outcome can be painful, it is much better for both individuals when the subject is discussed with honesty and compassion. It also is a more mature and responsible alternative to the conflict and the turmoil that may otherwise arise when the real issues are not confronted.

Chapter 8
Sex and Intimacy

Physical intimacy is a very important component of a healthy, loving relationship. The quality of such intimacy often reflects both the trust and emotional alliance of that partnership. For this reason, we often hear that most relationship problems can be found in the bedroom. While some people report that they can separate their sexual feelings from their emotional feelings, tension or conflict in a relationship frequently impacts both the frequency and quality of physical intimacy. Similarly, a person's self-image influences his capacity to freely and comfortably engage in sexual intimacy.

Being in a relationship with someone who has bipolar disorder presents challenges for emotional intimacy and the maintenance of a satisfying sexual relationship. The good news is that it is still possible to have a healthy sex life when loving someone with bipolar disorder.

All Relationships Have Sex/Intimacy Issues

Let's begin by placing your bond with your bipolar partner within the larger framework of relationships to see how these relationships are influenced by societal views regarding sex. As children we receive a wide range of messages about sex from our parents, relatives, religion, community, peers, and media. Many of the messages may seem confusing—and contradictory.

These guidelines often reflect mixed messages about what is sexually appropriate. Some religions emphasize procreation as the primary reason for sex and instill guilt for the pleasure we associate with sexual intimacy. We receive other messages that emphasize the importance of postponing sex until marriage, and still others that encourage young men to be sexually active as a way of proving their masculinity. If we pay attention to media reports, we would think that people are having sex everywhere and around-the-clock. By contrast, actual studies of sexual behavior suggest that while many people are leading a very active sex life, the numbers do not compare with what is depicted by the media.

The mixed messages we receive about sex as children serve to heighten our confusion about our sexuality as adults. It is no wonder that partaking in sexual intimacy provokes a wide range of expectations and emotions that foster or inhibit the development of healthy physical intimacy.

CASE STUDY: Richard and Pam

Richard and Pam's seven-year marriage showcases a number of complex issues that can arise regarding intimacy and sexuality in the bipolar relationship. Pam had known Richard for more than a year prior to their being married and was aware of his bipolar illness. The couple sought counseling after an escalation in Richard's sexual activities that undermined the sense of trust that Pam had worked hard to maintain. Although they experienced a very satisfactory and active sex life early in their relationship, the frequency and quality of physical intimacy had greatly diminished over the last several years. Pam had initiated couples counseling as a last resort to maintain their relationship.

To a great extent Pam blamed herself for the diminished interest in intimacy. However, as she came to understand, much of her decreased libido resulted from feelings of hurt and disappointment triggered by the feeling that Richard wasn't fully present for her. In part, this occurred because of Richard's bouts of mania and depression. Simultaneously he had seemed to distance himself from her, partly as a result of his difficulty with being assertive about many areas of their shared life. Since he was unable to state what he really wanted, Richard became resentful of Pam, which fueled her sense of rejection and their mutual withdrawal from each other.

Although he struggled to be faithful to Pam, Richard developed an interest in Internet pornography. Pam discovered this activity and, while she confronted him once, she soon accepted his actions and blamed herself for not being physically available to him. She rationalized that at least he wasn't having an affair, and she focused on the many positive aspects of their relationship. Still, Pam suffered a profound blow to her ego and a disappointment that triggered a growing sense of alienation.

Only after Pam discovered that her husband had sought contacts with women on the Internet did she become angry enough to threaten divorce if he did not accept individual and couples counseling. At first Richard minimized his activities by telling Pam that he only fantasized about contacting women. Then, he recanted and admitting to sexual contacts with several of the women, although he had not become romantically involved with any of them.

This pattern of dealing with issues of intimacy can occur in any relationship, but the quickness to act on sexual impulses is a major challenge for many individuals with bipolar disorder. It can be especially challenging when the nonbipolar partner behaves like Pam, fearful of conflict and feeling overly responsible for or overly understanding of her partner's behaviors. As an outcome of therapy, Richard and Pam became much more comfortable sharing their respective feelings. Richard made a commitment to the relationship, and Pam made the commitment to temporarily suspend any distrust while hoping they would reestablish their mutual faith.

Intimacy Does Not Always Equal Sex

A fulfilling sexual relationship can be a vital part of a healthy relationship. If you and your partner enjoy an active sex life despite the many distractions of everyday life, you are one of the fortunate ones. On the other hand, if competing demands on your life begin to interfere with your relationship, it may be time to reassess your priorities.

As a relationship evolves, the desire for sexual intimacy may vary, but it is only a problem when one partner desires intimacy more than the other. Too frequently couples become complacent and neglect to keep their sex life exciting. Other times, the pressure of parenthood causes problems. When a doting parent becomes overly focused on raising children, she may inadvertently neglect the romantic aspect of her relationship with her partner. For other partners, being part of a family may replace or compete with feeling fully comfortable with one's sexuality. You may soon experience a sense of familial connection like the one you experienced with your family of origin. A sense of family love soon dominates and distracts from the focus of any physical desire for intimacy.

Since differences in desire for sexual intimacy can lead to tension in a relationship, each couple must decide how best to address the issue. You may also want to engage the help of a marriage counselor or a sex therapist. It is important to remember that a couple can grow to value their relationship in many ways, and what works for one couple may not work for another. Even a hearty sex life may be based on a dysfunctional relationship, so sex alone is not the key to a successful bond.

Sex Does Not Always Equal Intimacy

People often forget that sex can be a way of avoiding intimacy. The classic story of the man who seeks sex with a prostitute to avoid the real issues at home with his wife is a good example. Some people shy away entirely from intimate relationships, preferring more casual associations and the one-night stand to satisfy their sexual urge.

ASK THE DOCTOR

How important is intimacy in my sex life?

During and after sex, do you feel closer to your partner? Or do you secretly wait for it to be over with, or wish it were happening some other way? Do you love your partner despite the way he performs in bed? Physical intimacy can take many forms and it is a vital part of a loving relationship. However, it can be most fulfilling when it is grounded in the emotional intimacy that allows each partner to be fully present with the other.

Some couples use sex as a way of making up after an argument. But sex alone is a poor substitute for conversation and will not reveal the root of their problem. Some couples come to expect this pattern and will pick a fight just to have sex as if their sexual intimacy serves to validate their partner's love. When sex is used as a form of reassurance for the partner who feels abandoned or is the target of her partner's anger, it camouflages a weakened relationship. Other couples may be going through the motions of sex because they feel they "must," but one or both parties are present in body only. Their minds are elsewhere, thinking about another person or some mundane chore they need to do on the following day.

Can you see how many people wrongly equate sex with intimacy and intimacy with sex? Even if your partner was not bipolar the two of you would still more than likely experience sexual issues.

Medications and Sex Drive

Some medications prescribed for bipolar illness can diminish both sexual desire and performance, and even those that don't may still adversely affect your bipolar partner in terms of his sexual appetite. Let's look at the big picture as far as medication is concerned:

1. Given the complex interconnectedness of human physiology, it is possible for any drug (including alcohol) to have some impact on the user's performance or sexual appetite. Alcohol, for example, can lessen inhibitions, but it can also inhibit male potency.
2. People who live with bipolar disorder are not the only ones who are prescribed antidepressants or other medications that inhibit sex drive. People take antidepressants for problems other than bipolar disorder.
3. Not all people are adversely affected by the sexual side effects of a given medication, as no drug affects everyone the same way.
4. A person's memory can be faulty or selective. Although medication can lead to sexual dysfunction, sometimes the user of a particular drug was already experiencing sexual issues before taking the drug in question.

5. Antidepressants are not the only drugs that may cause sexual side effects. Some people are also affected by antipsychotic medication. Moreover, drugs prescribed for high blood pressure (antihypertensives) and high cholesterol have also been reported to reduce sexual desire and/or performance.
6. The aging factor has a debilitating effect on sexual performance and desire. We are not implying that seniors no longer seek or enjoy sex, but everyone experiences a normal decrease in sexual activity as they age. A woman reaches her sexual peak during her middle twenties and experiences the earliest changes of her libido (sex drive) at midlife. The male libido peaks at age eighteen and begins its decline after age forty-five, the time when a man's level of testosterone begins to decrease. However, some seniors experience diminished interest because they feel inadequate and less sexually appealing then they were at an earlier age. Discomfort with their changing bodies alters their self-image, which makes some people shun physical intimacy. For others, life experience and shifting priorities can also play a role.

If your bipolar partner does not seem to have a strong interest in physical intimacy, you may want to put it in perspective. Many other factors besides the impact of medications may lead to a diminished sex drive.

Drugs to Increase Sexual Performance

The most common drugs prescribed for enhancing sexual performance and desire in men are Viagra, Cialis, and Levitra. However, since these drugs tend not to be covered by health insurance plans they can be very expensive. It's important that your doctor knows what other medications your partner is taking before a sexual enhancer is prescribed. These medications may have side effects and potentially negative interactions when combined with other medications.

Some men report that herbal remedies such as ginseng, horny goat, and yohimbe bark extract enhance their libido. Still, it should be emphasized that herbal remedies depend on their stimulating properties. Some preparations, like yohimbe bark extract, can induce high blood pressure and anxiety and, as a result, have become illegal in certain countries. Your bipolar partner should be wary of taking any substance that increases the potential for anxiety and should consult with his doctor before taking any herbal remedies.

WORD TO THE WISE

Enjoy Intimacy

Some people think of "sex" in terms of "orgasms." However, physical contact can still be mutually pleasurable and signal intimacy even with the failure to achieve orgasm. Kissing, touching, and caressing are also enjoyable and sexy.

For women, estrogen therapy is sometimes used to enhance sexual desire by increasing blood flow to the vagina. Progesterone can also be combined with the estrogen. Although women have lower amounts of testosterone than men, it is reported that testosterone plays a role in female sexual performance.

Since some people are uncomfortable discussing their concerns about sex with their physician, many are turning to the Internet for information about medications and herbal supplements. But, this can be harmful because of their potential negative side effects. Before beginning any new drug regimen, it is important that you and your partner openly discuss this with your doctor. Also, whether your partner is taking an over-the-counter herb or a prescription, it is advisable to have his blood pressure regularly checked since these treatments often work on the premise of stimulating the bloodstream. If your partner suffers from high blood pressure, he's less likely to be given a prescription drug of this type.

A wide variety of medications and alternative therapies is available today, and, since your relationship with a bipolar partner is not a unique phenomenon, several choices of treatment are available that can help increase your partner's sexual drive or performance. If affordable and your partner is able to take them, you may improve the satisfaction of your physical intimacy. But if these drugs are not an option, you may need to explore alternative forms of intimacy.

Other Factors

Some people feel that they must be in a particular frame of mind, or "in the mood," to have sex. The more diversions and responsibilities that we assume in our daily lives, the greater the demands that compete for our time. The desire for sex is diminished when other pursuits are prioritized. If you or your partner brings work home from the office, even mentally, your attention is otherwise diverted and you're less likely to be in the mood for sexual intimacy. If you work from home it can be difficult to switch gears from business matters to time spent alone with your partner. You may be mulling over some unresolved problem, or mentally planning your next day's schedule. Or, you and your partner may find yourselves talking in bed about the needs and activities of your children rather than sharing intimate moments together. Perhaps, by the time you begin preparing for bed, you're too fatigued for anything other than sleep.

During a manic episode your partner may have an increased sexual drive, but simultaneously her thoughts may be taking her in all different directions. Think about the last time you were disinterested in sex and had trouble falling asleep because you could not stop thinking about the kids or the checkbook or getting the car fixed; then, multiply the intensity of such rumination by ten. That is what goes on in your bipolar partner's head.

ASK THE DOCTOR

What are some chronic reasons for diminished sexual interest?

Other common causes for diminished sexual desire include anemia, diabetes, infections, a history of sexual abuse, conflicts regarding sexual identity or sexual orientation, and shyness or reservations about sex.

At the other extreme, remember the last time you were too exhausted for sex and double or triple the fatigue you experienced. This may give you some indication of how your bipolar partner feels when her medication dulls her out. Engaging sexually in this frame of mind may seem to be a daunting task rather than an enjoyable and nurturing activity.

Keep in mind that depression plays havoc on a person's sex life. Think about the last time you felt sad. If you sought comfort through sex, you were probably disappointed as it most likely failed to lift your mood. Perhaps you even wanted to be alone. Many factors, unrelated to medication, may influence your bipolar partner's moods and make him unresponsive to sex.

CASE STUDY: Marsha and Peter

Diminished libido may also be the outcome for a partner who experiences frequent disappointment, rejection, or, worse, ridicule and shaming based on what her partner says or does. When extreme, such hurt may even lead to the avoidance of touch as an expression of intimacy. This was Marsha's experience with her husband, Peter, whom she described as becoming increasingly critical of her in the recent years of their marriage.

Marsha says, "We were together for several years before getting married. I knew he had bipolar disorder. I also knew he could be somewhat irritable and, yes, there were times when he seemed quick to criticize or devalue me. But, for the most part, we enjoyed a wonderful relationship. Our sexual life was great and we were quite affectionate.

"As time passed, however, he seemed to become increasingly mean and critical. He would put me down for the way I cooked a dinner, for my selection of clothing—even for my choice of friends. I attributed his behavior to the bipolar illness and, over time, I became uncomfortable saying anything to him since I was afraid of making him even more upset. Gradually, I found myself lacking any desire to be physically intimate with him. I must admit that, in hindsight, my lack of desire was the impetus for his further withdrawal and increased irritability. The more difficult he became to live with, the less interested I was in touching him, until I shunned any form of physical contact with the man whom I had once loved so deeply."

Marsha sought counseling because she truly wanted to work on the marriage, but she was too timid to acknowledge to Peter how strongly she had been impacted by his behavior. Marsha later said, "I blamed Peter's illness for his behavior. I've never been able to assertively express my feelings, especially anger. Actually, I was feeling hurt but thought it my duty to try harder to satisfy him."

Together, Marsha and Peter were playing out their feelings without openly addressing them. In time, his criticism led to her withdrawal and, ultimately, to his abandonment, which precipitated a buildup of isolation. This pattern intensified as Peter began to seek physical intimacy outside of his marriage. While this dance can occur in any relationship, Peter's bipolar illness was in large part responsible for his unfaithfulness.

When Marsha discovered Peter's infidelity, she was quick to minimize her pain and anger because of her ongoing struggle with self-worth. Her discomfort regarding sex—even touching—stemmed from an escalating sense of hurt and shame, and the feeling of inadequacy about not measuring up to Peter's expectations. Although unaware of her subliminal feelings, Marsha had become disgusted with Peter. Through therapy, Marsha gradually regained a sense of trust and was able to express her feelings for Peter. As an outgrowth of her self-awareness and improved self-confidence, Marsha committed herself to work on salvaging the marriage. As a contingency for staying together, with which Peter agreed to comply, Marsha demanded that he consent to couples counseling and individual therapy to work out his degrading behavior toward her.

When Sex Seems Out of Control

Many people immediately identify fidelity as a major component in their relationship. While some partners may engage in physical intimacy outside of their committed relationships, the bipolar partner is more vulnerable to having an affair than his nonbipolar counterpart. Sexual acting out is a common symptom of mania and, in the throes of mania, sexually compulsive behavior can be about the need to prove one's grandiosity. Sex is a way of feeling worshipped or admired. A word of caution: remember that your partner may seek intimacy with a con artist or someone who is physically violent, has a sexually transmitted disease, or does not practice safe sex. Besides the normal hurt and anger that is the aftermath of infidelity, your bipolar partner may be endangering both of your lives.

The signs of infidelity may include your partner working late hours at the office, mysterious weekend "business" or "fishing" trips, sudden gifts of guilt, and so on. If the mania is severe, perhaps no explanation will be offered and your partner will instead make it seem like you are the one who is nosey and critical. Since mania triggers paranoia and feelings of persecution, your partner may even try to argue that you drove him to it or that you are going to use this against him in a divorce and take him for every penny he is worth. He may even accuse *you* of being unfaithful.

You may feel uncomfortable distrusting your partner and subsequently ignore the evidence that he may be acting out sexually. This may increase your distrust still further and lead you to feel even more isolated and resentful. Your concerns need to be expressed, and the best approach is one that emphasizes your hurt and genuine caring in addition to the anger you understandably may experience.

It's also possible that you will become the target of your partner's heightened sexual interest. This may be challenging at a time when your trust is diminished or when your partner is behaving in ways that make you want to withdraw. Being cajoled, accused, or name-called into another round of sex may signal the onslaught of sexual mania. At the same time, it may also be an opportune time to openly discuss how to spice up your sex life. An honest discussion can enhance the trust you experience with each other.

If explicit requests for sex reach a point that they violate your comfort zone, the problem may be as simple as a lack of sleep. You also may not be in the mood for sex, or your partner may demand things you don't want to do. Your personal needs must also be respected, and under no circumstances should you feel you must comply with any sex act that might be unsafe. Depending on the specifics of your partner's bipolar symptoms, you may even fear exposing yourself to a sexually transmitted disease—especially if you know that he has been sexually active with other people. If you and your partner have already had sex after you discover he has had a sexual liaison with another person, both of you may want to be tested for HIV.

If your partner is in the throes of a severe manic episode, call her doctor or take her to the hospital. If your partner suffers from hypomania (mild mania) and little can be done medically to treat her, try to initiate a new strategy of open communication about such matters. You might say, "I'm tired," or "I'd rather not do that," and hope that your needs will be respected as in any other relationship. Failing this, you might try to suggest that both of you get some sleep or perhaps substitute a massage for sex so your partner still feels connected and loved. You might also try to distract her with interesting conversation, a book, a computer game, or even some comfort food—whatever it is that you feel she might enjoy.

If your partner engages in sexually risky behavior, you may feel that you have no choice but to end the relationship, or you may accept the risk and stay committed. If you choose the latter, seek couples counseling and make it clear to your partner that this kind of behavior will not be tolerated again.

It Takes Two

Intimacy between partners is possible even if your sex life faces challenges over time. It requires the honest effort of both of you, and your willingness to express your own needs while carefully listening to those of your partner. You may sometimes feel completely responsible for the success or failure of your relationship, including the quality of your sex life, but in reality in every relationship—including your bipolar relationship—both partners share equal responsibility for the quality of that relationship. If your partner's symptoms are reasonably under control, it is possible to have a mutually fulfilling sex life.

Even if your partner's sexual behavior is out of control, it still takes the two of you to figure things out. If you know your partner acts out sexually with others and you cannot tolerate this, it is *her* responsibility to adjust her behavior or face the consequences. If she continues to make sexual demands that you cannot meet and that you find upsetting, then your only option might be to end the relationship.

You should also understand that your partner's bipolar condition does not exclude her from expressing her own feelings and thoughts regarding sex. Nor does being bipolar offer any excuse or in any way diminish her responsibility as an equal partner. Like all other couples, it is wise to approach these matters with a sense of compassion and respect for human fallibility.

Many couples have mixed attitudes about the role of sex in their relationship. Even the importance of sex to each partner may vary from time to time. Some couples engage regularly in sex, while others are content to have sex less frequently. Although a fulfilling sexual relationship should be an important consideration for every healthy relationship, you will face unusual challenges by loving someone with bipolar disorder. The choices you make should be arrived at mutually, but only after individual reflection on what is most important to each of you. During this process, remember not to be too hard on yourselves if you are one of the many couples who remain baffled by sex.

PART III

DAY TO DAY WITH BIPOLAR DISORDER

While it may sound redundant, we need to emphasize that bipolar disorder is a chronic illness. This means that while your partner may have days, weeks, months, or even years without major exacerbation of symptoms, you will both be challenged on a daily basis to address the special concerns of living with this disorder. This section focuses on helping you to meet this challenge. This includes attending to daily routines around the house as well as being aware of how raising a family may be impacted when your partner has this illness. It also involves being prepared to respond to your partner and children if your partner suffers a major episode. What to prioritize in your relationship and how to best take care of yourself are two key concerns that also require mindful attention on a daily basis.

Chapter 9
Can You Have a Normal Household?

"Normal" can mean many things and is often a subjective concept. Many individuals report coming from a "normal" home environment in spite of some very serious and destructive family behaviors. The fictional Addams Family considered itself a normal family with a normal household, and why not? All their family members appear happy and share the same strong values. So, if by "normal" you mean a household devoid of tension and turmoil, the answer is yes! A "normal" household can be yours—although sometimes it will be easier to achieve this goal than others.

Financial Issues

We have discussed financial issues in relation to symptoms of mania and how these issues impact the trust you have in your partner. The focus now is on how you can protect yourself and your relationship from the potential financial hardships that can occur when living with a bipolar partner. The following specific strategies can be practiced on a day-to-day basis.

Spend a Little Time to Save a Lot

A major financial challenge you may face in your relationship is ensuring your partner stays within the budget that you—as a couple—agree upon (during his most stable period). You may want to seek the assistance of an attorney to achieve this goal. Specifically, an attorney can help you form an agreement which specifies that your bipolar partner cannot spend, sell, give away, or trade past a certain monetary amount without your signature. If you cannot afford an attorney, see if free or low-cost legal help is available in your community. The nearest law school may also have students who are eager for legal experience. When initiating this action, you may feel uneasy or guilty about setting limits or anxiety that your partner will react with anger. Remember that it will be easier to secure a commitment from your partner if you engage him in an open and frank discussion.

If your partner cannot work or has proven to be a serious financial risk, you can set up a fixed weekly or monthly allowance. If given weekly, she may be less likely to impulsively spend large amounts at once, but it may also make her more likely to ask for "advances." Whatever plan you follow, you must remain firm.

Limit your credit cards so you can monitor your expenses more closely. You may, for example, avoid obtaining credit cards from retail businesses and keep only one or two cards that will be accepted for most purchases. Additionally, even if you qualify for high credit lines, keep your credit cards and bank overdraft lines at low levels. Maintaining an accurate record of your liquid assets and limiting them will also make it less likely that your bipolar partner will overspend. Keep in mind that while you want to avoid becoming preoccupied with the worst-case scenarios, these strategies may be important should your bipolar partner impulsively decide to divorce you with no forewarning.

Other Bipolar Traits and Money

While forgetfulness is common for everyone, it's most identifiable in bipolar patients because of the symptoms associated with the disorder and/or the medications. Your partner may forget conversations you had five minutes ago about money, to note a check he wrote, or the fact that he used the credit card. If, at times, you think that your partner is forgetting on purpose, this is an issue of honesty that needs to be addressed. However, if his forgetfulness occurs frequently, you should be mindful not to immediately draw this conclusion. Meanwhile, you may want to further curtail your partner's access to finances if he cannot remember what was discussed.

ASK THE DOCTOR

Could my partner have attention deficit hyperactivity disorder?

People with a diagnosis of bipolar disorder are more likely than others to also have attention deficit hyperactivity disorder (ADHD). This may include difficulties with concentration, impulsiveness, and distractibility, all symptomatic of forgetfulness.

Another problem that may arise during a financial discussion is your bipolar partner's manic tendency to talk a lot, and in very complex ways. A simple question like, "Did you bounce a check?" can turn into a confusing verbal epic of knots and tangles. There is a good chance that extending the conversation at such a time may simply add to the chaos. It may, instead, be helpful to have your partner write down what he is trying to say. Tell him outright that you cannot follow his conversation, so he needs to jot it down. Having the time and solitude to put his answer in writing may allow your partner an opportunity for increased concentration and a reduction in emotionality that can arise when questioned about how the money was spent. Similarly, it will spare you the frustration of having a conversation that may seem convoluted and difficult to follow. After you read your partner's letter, give yourself some time and space, perhaps even sleep on it, in the effort to sort through possible contradictions and superfluous information. Your response should be brief.

At times, you may provide a structured request rather than an open-ended inquiry for information. For example, requesting that your partner enter a log of expenses that includes the amount spent, the date, the purpose, and a two-sentence description may spare you the frustration of reading a multipage document of a detailed expenditure. If contradictions exist, you can then be more focused in your request for further information. By cutting through the nonsense and keeping things simple, you will be able to put the matter to rest.

WORD TO THE WISE:
Set Money Aside

When playing the game "Monopoly" some players put a $500 bill under the board at the start of the game so they will have extra money when needed. Silly as it may seem, once the game gets going it is easy to forget about the $500, which may come in handy when the player needs additional funds. Likewise, it's important in the real world to have money set aside in case of an emergency and to plan according to your specific needs.

If Your Partner Works

Whenever both partners earn an income, they are faced with the task of deciding how to best manage their shared earnings. Although a challenge for any couple, this is especially important when your partner has bipolar disorder. One of the main decisions you'll need to make is what percentage of the paycheck should be deposited into your joint accounts. Many couples resolve the issue by setting up three accounts: an individual account for each partner and a joint account to which each contributes an identical percentage of their earnings. While this financial arrangement may be suitable for most couples, giving your partner access to a joint account may not provide you with the financial security you need. If this is the case, you may want to refer to the recommendations at the beginning of this chapter or place a cap on the amount of money in your joint account while you maintain control over the remaining difference.

Your partner may argue that it is her money and doesn't belong to anyone else. Should this occur, gently remind her that the money belongs to both of you, your children, and other family members when needed. Reassure your partner that you are keeping the money safe for everyone to enjoy together.

Job Stress and the Home

It is common for everyone to experience stress in the workplace, and it's also common to take work-related tension out on those with whom we live. With a bipolar partner, it is important to remain vigilant to this—and the level of stress your partner is experiencing—because of the impact it could have on your relationship. For example, your partner may experience periods of time during which all of his energy is focused to meet the demands of his job. During these times he may have little energy for anything else and might devote an entire weekend to regroup and maintain the level of energy required for the week ahead.

While each of us may, at times, experience an escalation in work-related stress, it deserves increased attention if it becomes a pattern with your partner. This may reflect increased demands of the workplace, but also a diminished capacity to handle ongoing stress due to some impending depressive episode. Addressing this reaction early on may significantly reduce the likelihood of an episode or the intensity of one should it occur.

Occasions may also arise when everyone brings stress about specific tasks and their deadlines home from their workplace. This may happen more frequently if the job is particularly meaningful. With bipolar disorder, minimal or moderate levels of stress are favored. It's best if the job is one that will not lead your partner to have more than an occasional worrisome night. Air traffic controllers, police officers, or even social workers who deal with abuse cases all deal with high levels of stress. If your partner is choosing a first career or job, bear in mind the potential challenges and level of stress associated with that choice. Even the most interesting job may be unsuitable for your partner if it involves major shifts in the workload with impending deadlines, overtime, and confrontation with difficult people—coworkers and/or supervisors.

Because of the demands of the workplace, people with bipolar disorder often do well when self-employed. They can manage their own schedules while working in the area most suitable to their individual talent and interest level, be it freelance writing, consulting, or a home-based business. However, working at home has its own challenges. To maintain a healthy relationship, both partners must establish acceptable parameters. Another problem confronted by the person who works from home is the isolated environment. Although writers usually prefer a secluded setting, people in other professions may find the solitude of working at home very lonely. In addition, distractions caused by children or even the family pet can be disruptive. For someone with bipolar disorder, the benefits often outweigh the disadvantages, and the responsibility falls on both partners to confront the challenges and resolve them together.

CASE STUDY: Christopher and Mary

Working from home can be challenging, as Christopher, a thirty-five-year-old literary agent well knows. For Christopher, developing the self-discipline required to avoid working excessive hours was a large hurdle. He says, "It's so hard to stop in the middle of an interesting writing project, the review of a new manuscript, or even the occasional editing project. Also, website updates and our monthly newsletter are sometimes delegated to evening hours since the normal business day is filled with phone calls and project submissions." However, these excessive working hours can result in poor health and discord in the relationship unless these occurrences are kept to a minimum.

Christopher admits to having trouble putting his work down due to his passionate interest in the publishing industry. He often picks up a manuscript and remains riveted to the chair. Sometimes he looks up hours after he's supposed to have finished working and realizes that he's accomplished little else. He says, "Since manuscripts and book proposals arrive daily, it's easy to fall behind without enforcing some measure of self-discipline. For a person who lives with bipolar disorder, managing a business while monitoring an illness can be quite an undertaking. Especially since I'm working with authors and publishers in different time zones, my normal business day begins on Eastern time and ends on Pacific time."

Christopher's two sons are both adults with families of their own, but his wife Mary's life is impacted by his long and erratic working hours. When dinner is served late, Christopher tries to compensate by preparing special meals. But hardest of all is knowing when to quit for the day, as Christopher usually returns to his office before bedtime to "check e-mail." He admits that he has trouble putting down work:

"Whereas I can function on less than five or six hours of sleep, Mary requires a minimum of seven hours. 'What's taking so long?' she'll ask when my e-mail check stretches beyond the anticipated amount of time. 'Just one more e-mail and I'm done,' I reply, and if I don't make it in time Mary goes to sleep without me. Still, as an avid reader, she knows to expect that when I do come to bed it's with a book in hand. I wait until she's sleeping before switching on the nightlight, and then read until I fall asleep. Fortunately, the low light is adequate for reading and doesn't disturb Mary's rest."

Help Around the House

Every couple that shares a household faces the challenge of chores essential to maintaining their home. Whether these tasks involve cleaning, cooking, organizing, or decorating, it is important that couples discuss how they will address their household duties. Frequently one partner may, without fanfare, assume responsibility for certain duties without discussing them with his mate. Others may find that listing each chore and who will attend to them is the most effective way to balance the household duties. If both are content with their respective chores there will be little conflict, but some couples take on tasks that they grow to resent and then fail to discuss their feelings with each other. The mounting tension that inevitably results can be damaging to any relationship.

Similarly, it is important to emphasize that people, whether bipolar or not, may have very different standards and different priorities regarding how clean or organized their home must be. As in any partnership, if harmony is to prevail, some compromise must be met. If you have a strong need for cleanliness and bristle if crumbs are left on the table, it's important to remember that your mate does not have to maintain the same standards unless she agrees to do so. Your partner is not responsible for your anxiety, nor does her attitude mean that she does not love or respect you. Don't be resentful at such moments and pick up the crumbs. You need to be responsible for maintaining your own standards if your partner is neither available to or does not wish to maintain them. Remember that when their differing attitudes are extreme, even nonbipolar couples split up over such issues.

If your bipolar partner's symptoms are under control, household duties should be shared. Even if one of you is a full-time homemaker, extra tasks that require an extra pair of hands may pile up. Conversely, if your partner's symptoms are not always under control, even basic household chores can pose a serious problem. Always maintain realistic expectations of your partner during these periods.

WORD TO THE WISE

Share Housecleaning Duties

In today's world, women still assume more housecleaning duties than men even when both the man and the woman are employed outside the home. If your bipolar partner is hung up on gender stereotypes, you might see this behavior amplified around the house. A bipolar woman might be fanatical about keeping the house clean while a bipolar man may insist that housework is only for women. But, this may not apply if your mate is less conservative about gender norms.

Household Extremes

Given the extreme nature of mood shifts in bipolar disorder, your bipolar partner, at times, may be obsessively neat or exceptionally sloppy. Periods of mania may be accompanied by a frenetic level of cleaning and organizing. Alternatively, her mania may foster disorganization when she is simultaneously involved in several projects but isn't capable of completing any of them. In the midst of a deep depression, she may be too lethargic to accomplish even the simplest tasks. When your partner is more stable, her attitude should more accurately reflect her true preferences.

Excessive Neatness

You may think, "Gee, what is wrong with someone who loves to keep a clean house?" (Or maintain a perfectly trimmed lawn or the shiniest hand polished car?) True, most people would rather live in a clean home than a dirty one, and if someone other than you wants to keep it that way . . . what's the problem? Such organization may be manageable and reflects a constructive way to channel energy. However, fanatical housecleaning can be a symptom of mania or escalating mania or it could precipitate high levels of stress that will set a manic attack in motion.

A clean kitchen floor is nice, but a speck of dust does not mean the floor must be scrubbed with a toothbrush. Enjoyable and hygienic as a clean environment can be, fanaticism makes others unhappy and nervous and the cleaner is missing the point of maintaining a household. If the home is not the place where family members experience love and peace, then the home is merely a dwelling.

During a manic mood the "crisis" of spilling some milk on the floor can lead to an episode of anger, despair, and frustration. Such accidents may trigger intense feelings of inadequacy and even acting out. When this happens, your partner should be reminded that he is not in complete control of his life. It is the emotional intensity associated with your partner's focus on cleaning that signals a compulsion rather than just the inclination toward cleanliness and neatness.

This intensity may be reflected when your partner gets carried away doing something, and his intensity brings out the opposite of what he was attempting to do in the first place. For example, he mops the floor and becomes so frustrated that he hurls the bucket against a window and breaks it. She may stay up all night sewing new curtains for the living room, and the next morning cut them up into little pieces. In the throes of mania, such behavior is in keeping with the bipolar sufferer's vacillating moods and impaired judgment.

CASE STUDY: Carmen and Miguel

Rooted in our deepest caring and devotion for a loved one is a powerful desire to reduce their pain. Empathy allows us to experience our loved one's anguish, and compassion moves us to alleviate it. This was the driving force for Miguel, whose wife, Carmen, had been diagnosed with bipolar illness two years after their wedding. His concern for Carmen intensified when she seemed overwhelmed by an obsessive concern for household chores during periods of mania. Carmen was generally well organized and conscientious about keeping her home neat and clean, but went overboard when manic and was quick to demand that Miguel be as fastidious as she. "I saw how anxious she was, and I wanted to help her feel better," said Miguel. "Sure, I like a neat home, but I don't care as much as she does about always keeping it perfectly clean. I agreed to help until I got sick of it."

Miguel gradually became increasingly resentful about devoting what he considered a disproportionate amount of time to tasks that he did not value as strongly as his wife. Additionally, she conveyed in words and behavior that his lack of compliance reflected an underlying disinterest in her.

Miguel felt held hostage by her grip on him and his resulting desire to satisfy her, but his behavior was grounded by the fear of conflict and tension.

He says, "What really pushed me over the edge was her request that I alphabetize the canned goods in our pantry and the cleaning solutions in the utility closet! While I momentarily agreed, my resentment developed into outrage and I now regret my reaction. I not only refused to do what she asked, but I responded with a barrage of anger and shaming and devaluing comments. She did not deserve it."

It took a series of these outbursts for Miguel and Carmen to seek counseling. Within the context of their sessions they were helped to recognize that loving someone does not mean that you must feel subservient. A loving relationship involves compromise. Miguel was helped to feel more comfortable in assertively stating his limits regarding Carmen's requests. Simultaneously, Carmen learned to recognize that Miguel's refusal to comply with her every wish did not suggest a lack concern for her. Although she needed to convey her anxieties to Miguel, it was unrealistic to expect him to jump at her every whim.

A heightened tendency toward obsessiveness may not always accompany an episode of mania. In a more severe manic state, your partner may suddenly decide that the living room should be painted an array of colors accented with red polka dots, or that pictures from old magazines should be glued to the wall. Perhaps, he'll decide that your house really needs a larger living room and suddenly, without discussion, you return home to find the wall between the living room and the den has been knocked down. Such extreme examples reflect a severe impairment of judgment that requires immediate attention. If an incident like this occurs, consult your partner's doctor.

If your bipolar loved one appears overwhelmed by the chores, it may be a good idea to lighten her load. Either assume more responsibility yourself or, if affordable, perhaps pay someone to come in and clean once a week. Try to find other activities for your partner, including spending more quality time with you. If your partner cannot sit still or slow down, a phone call to the doctor might be in order.

Excessive Sloppiness

At the other extreme, it can be terribly annoying to live with someone who never picks up after himself. He enters a room and within a short time it becomes cluttered with empty grocery bags, candy bar wrappers, and clothes on the floor. If he goes into the kitchen for even a glass of water, he creates a mess and neglects to clean it up. Or, if he attempts to clean it up, he creates a bigger mess.

ASK THE DOCTOR

Is my partner's lack of organization due to bipolar disorder?

Keep in mind that a lack of attention to cleaning and organizing may be due to factors other than depression or mania. Your partner may be accustomed to having others attend to the basic chores of daily living if that was the way he was raised. Or, it may be an attention deficit problem that has not been diagnosed. For others, attending to household chores may be low priority as compared to other life goals and activities.

Keep in mind that depression creates the disinclination to care about order and cleanliness. Mania, on the other hand, creates chaos, and in a manic state a person can have many interests simultaneously and the next thing you know stuff is everywhere: stacks of magazines or newspapers, an old aquarium in need of cleaning, and so on. When severe, there is no suggestion of order at all. Clothes are mixed up with old pizza boxes, which are mixed up with broken CD cases, and disorder abounds.

ASK THE DOCTOR

Could other conditions be contributing?

If your bipolar partner has other conditions that may limit her ability to carry out specific chores, such as dyslexia (a learning disability affecting reading, writing, or spelling) or dyspraxia (a neurological disorder impacting motor coordination), he may be poor at tasks that require following directions or good coordination, skills required to perform many household chores.

It would be nice if you could wave a magic wand and some power would intervene to instill your partner with a sense of responsibility for household chores. Unfortunately, that's not going to happen, but you can talk to your partner and even set aside time for a weekly discussion to identify which chores need attention. Together, create a list of the chores and who is to fulfill each one. Displaying this list in a high-traffic area of your home will increase the chances of it being noticed. Be sure to provide positive feedback regarding chores that are completed and your appreciation for your partner's efforts. Under some circumstances, you may playfully provide rewards as you might do with children who neglect their chores. The challenge in this strategy is that you not relate as a parent rewarding a child but as an equal truly appreciative of your partner's help.

Whatever choices you make, remember that negotiation of household chores is challenging for any couple, but the rewarding aspects of your relationship should overshadow any stress presented by such issues.

Communicating with Others

We have previously offered guidelines to help you and your partner communicate with each other. However, there are also considerations that deserve special attention when it comes to communicating with others. While addressing the unique demands of your relationship requires considerable time and energy, both of you need to communicate and maintain relationships with other people. Connections with other individuals become even more essential in light of the stress you may endure. If and when your partner requires hospitalization, a strong support system of family, friends, and associates will be welcome in helping you face the challenges that lie ahead.

It is unfortunate that some bipolar sufferers respond to their disorder with shame and embarrassment, which leads to their avoidance of other people. However, because of other's prejudices, the question remains, how much should you reveal about your partner's bipolar condition, and to whom? Conversely, might your partner disclose something about his condition that will cause you discomfort?

Telling Other People

As with other issues surrounding bipolar disorder, many of your decisions may be determined by how well your partner is doing. If she is responsive to treatment and displaying few symptoms, it may not be necessary to divulge any details about her bipolar condition. However, you may feel the need to discuss your situation for a variety of reasons. For instance, you might be inclined to share your challenges with a close friend or neighbor as you might disclose other aspects—both good and bad—of your life.

You may even want others to know about your partner in the effort to raise public awareness. They can see for themselves that a mental condition can be controlled and should not be a source of shame. You may even decide to discuss your circumstances as a way of dealing with your own anxiety, that gnawing concern that your situation will soon be discovered.

Unfortunately, there is no way to predict how other people will respond. The people who genuinely care about you should respond with compassion and understanding, but some—due to their own fears or ignorance—may have a negative reaction to your disclosure. They may be frightened to know that your partner is bipolar and may be fearful of being around if something bad happens. They may even be prejudiced against mental illness and think it is "beneath them" to be friends with someone who is mentally ill. Some may voice no reaction and others may be adamant about what they think you should do. In the extreme, a few may choose to sever all ties with you. People may also surprise you. Those you assume will be supportive may end up disappointing you, while others whom you think will be scared off might prove their loyalty.

If your partner displays at least some symptoms on a regular basis it would probably be wise to inform those closest to you about your partner's diagnosis. Otherwise, they may wrongly assume your partner is rude when her mania prevents them from getting a word in edgewise or that she is a snob when in fact she is severely depressed. People may also be annoyed when your partner fails to remember a conversation or angry when he yells at them over nothing. Although you cannot predict how people will accept the news, some might have already suspected that something was wrong. It is good for them to know that it is the illness they are seeing, rather than some personal affront.

You and your partner should arrive at a mutual decision whether or not to make her bipolar condition public. If your partner prefers not to disclose any information, you may want to honor her wishes by respecting her privacy. Be aware, however, that this may put you in an awkward position. For example, if your partner acts out in a frightening or embarrassing way at a dinner party it may be better to clear the air so that those present understand the origin of the problem. You may want to bring these types of occurrences to the attention of your partner's doctor. Make sure it is understood that you do not want the kind of life where you have to hide from other people and that you feel the truth would help set everyone at ease. This also requires that you be aware of any mixed feelings you may be harboring, perhaps your own shame or that somehow you will be blamed for the situation.

WORD TO THE WISE

Keep It Confidential

It is not uncommon for a partner to reveal pertinent information about his mate to a close friend or family member, even after promising to maintain confidentiality. It's also possible for a person to let something slip out and tell "just this one person." However, if your partner is firm about maintaining her privacy and you tell people anyway, don't be surprised if the facts get back to her.

If you do decide to tell other people, remember that while a support system is important for you to vent your feelings, nobody likes to listen to a broken record. If all you do is complain about your partner's bipolar disorder, people will tire of hearing about it. Some may withdraw, and others may even suggest you leave the relationship if you are so unhappy. You may also be confronted with the more intrusive comments and all kinds of questions, such as: "What's it like living with someone who's crazy?" or, "Can't she just take control of herself?" Try to distinguish between bad manners and genuine ignorance when you're faced with these kinds of remarks. Be especially mindful of facial expressions and body language: are they smirking and smug, or do they seem sympathetic?

WORD TO THE WISE

Find Your True Friends

You can learn a lot about who your true friends are when dealing with an illness like bipolar disorder. This does not mean that people who drop out of your life are "bad" people, but it does indicate that they cared less about you and are unavailable to share the difficult as well as the good times. In such cases, you may be better off without them.

Your Partner's Communication with Others

Since all people are flawed, so are human relationships flawed. Just as you have your own way of relating to and interacting with those around you, so does your bipolar partner. If Person B does not like something Person A just said, it is up to Person B to defend himself without your interference. Exceptions should be made for children, the elderly, and the infirm.

Be mindful that you cannot expect to control all aspects of your partner's life. If you obsessively worry that she will say something odd to the neighbors, or the "wrong thing" to your best friend, or act out her mania in front of a coworker, you may be doing the greatest harm to yourself. If, as a result of your partner's words or actions, your neighbors choose to avoid her, assume they know how to excuse themselves. Likewise, if your best friend was insulted by your partner, let her decide how to handle the situation unless she asks you for help. If your partner is acting manic or depressed in front of others, do not assume they are judging you negatively. Even if they are making a judgment call, it is their problem, not yours, and what they think may simply reflect their ignorance or fear.

If you are the recipient of your partner's insulting remark, let him know it. If a remark is made in a social situation, it may be wise to wait until afterwards before you say something. This is not because your partner is bipolar, but rather because your niece's wedding or your boss's birthday party is neither the time nor the place to reprimand him. Nor do you want others to expect to have to deal with some melodramatic scene whenever you and your partner are present.

WORD TO THE WISE

Find the Right Balance

If your bipolar partner is a real homebody, you may want to consult a doctor about how much social life he can comfortably handle. Bipolar disorder does not determine every aspect about a person, so your partner may benefit from a gentle nudge to get out in the world and meet people.

Some bipolar people are highly talented and charismatic and surround themselves with a wide social circle. Others are members of a support network and develop new friends through their group. Conversely, some people may find it difficult to be in the presence of your bipolar partner for any extended period of time. Your partner may become a reclusive coach potato, spending time only with you. He may also be one of those people with a lot of acquaintances but few real friends. Your partner's mania may be responsible for him spreading himself thinly across a wide social spectrum, and although many people know who he is, few may want to know him better.

In a normal relationship one's intimate partner is the most important person in his life, and your role may have even greater significance to your bipolar partner, especially if your partner has few regular social contacts and spends most of his time with you. Hopefully, this is a pleasure not a burden and you're also are attending to your needs for social contact and connection.

Asking for Help

Emphasizing our independence is an inherent part of our Western culture. In fact, we most often overemphasize it when we should instead be recognizing that we are truly interdependent, needing to rely on each other for some form of support throughout our lives. Every person needs help at some time and requesting it is not a sign of weakness. And while you may take pride in being able to manage many of the challenges of your relationship, asking for help may often be necessary. In this context, "asking for help" can mean two different things: asking your bipolar partner for help, or asking some other person(s) for help.

Asking Your Partner for Help

A thin line at times exists between realistically acknowledging the limitations that bipolar disorder can place on an individual and protecting her from assuming more than she can comfortably face. It's important to realize that all people bring strengths and weaknesses to a relationship. One might be a good cook, while the other excels at balancing the budget. If your partner is hopeless when it comes to vacuuming, you would agree to take on this chore. When it comes to dealing with the service people who support your life—the banker, phone service personnel, the remodeling consultant—you might be better at communicating with them than your partner.

Be alert to any tendencies that may cause you to overlook the help your partner can provide. Be mindful of taking on tasks or responsibilities that, while somewhat challenging to your partner, are ones that she can efficiently manage. Similarly, be alert to those times when you don't ask for help because you maintain unnecessarily high expectations for how a particular task should be handled. Whether it involves cooking a meal or tending to the garden, be open to asking for assistance.

Certainly in extreme cases, some bipolar individuals are incapable of handling anything other than the simplest of tasks. During a major depressive episode, even simple jobs may be too demanding and result in your partner feeling hopeless should he fail at the task. Similarly, if your partner is in a highly manic state you may receive more "help" than you bargained for!

Asking Others for Help

Children and other close relatives can help share the everyday burdens of running a family. However, it is important that children not be overburdened and are only given chores that are age appropriate, such as raking leaves or mowing the lawn. Their priorities should focus on keeping up with schoolwork and maintaining a healthy social life.

ASK THE DOCTOR

Who is likely to help out?

With an elderly relative, an illness, or some special needs, women offer to help more often than men. In recent years, however, men are increasingly taking on the role of caretaker as both men and women challenge the more traditional gender roles and embrace their potential for compassionate caretaking.

While family members may be available and willing to help out, if they feel overloaded they may be resentful. Even when you're feeling overwhelmed, be mindful that your relatives also have families of their own and other commitments. You don't want to be perceived as helpless or overly reliant on others.

Also, be cautious of the friend who appears overly eager to help. Even though she probably has the best of intentions, "helping out" should not be a substitute for an otherwise empty life. Perhaps she is lonely and needs to meet more people, or she may even be expecting something from you in return. A true friend will rally to your defense and come through with help and support but is also someone who feels comfortable enough to say, "Sorry, I'm going out of town tomorrow," or "I'd like to come over, but I have a date."

When money is involved and your bipolar partner has caused a huge debt, seek legal and financial advice. If you cannot afford professional consultation, obtain assistance from your local bank representative or through free or sliding-scale services. The Internet is another source of information, but always double-check any advice obtained online, because a lot of inaccurate sources are posted.

Caution should also be taken when borrowing money from family or friends, and it should be avoided whenever possible. It is wise to keep business matters separate from personal relationships. You might offer to reimburse a loan with interest, thereby treating it as a business agreement. It also will make you feel less indebted to the person from whom you are borrowing. Depending on the amount of cash involved, you might ask several people for smaller amounts rather than rely on one person for the entire lump sum. In this way you are not imposing too much on any one person, and it will be easier to reimburse people with smaller payments. Finally, put the agreement in writing for your mutual protection.

Living with a partner who has bipolar illness can present a broad range of day-to-day challenges, but the more strategies you identify in advance, the better prepared you will be to manage. Most importantly, you will help to ensure that you and your partner enjoy a more satisfying and loving relationship.

Chapter 10
Planning a Family

So what about having children? Is this okay to do when you have a bipolar partner? Does it involve special considerations? How might your bipolar partner react during and following a pregnancy? What might your concerns be at this time? The decision to have children raises many concerns for all couples. However, becoming parents when you are involved in a bipolar relationship can be especially challenging. Doing so requires that both of you are knowledgeable as well as emotionally prepared to address these unique issues.

Additionally, if you do decide to have children, the more informed you are about what bipolar illness means, what you can do about it, and your attitudes toward it, the more sensitive you will be to the needs of your partner, your children, yourself, and your family. How you relate with your partner regarding her illness will influence your child's attitudes toward the illness and his bipolar parent. Your child's relationship will also be influenced by what you directly express to him about your partner and her illness; the messages you convey in both words and actions will have a lasting affect on your child's acceptance of bipolar disorder.

Concerns about Having Children

There are numerous concerns that should be addressed if you and your partner wish to have children. Most of these concerns arise when the mother-to-be has bipolar illness. However, having to deal with your bipolar partner can also be an unusual stress for you if you are pregnant.

Will My Child Have Bipolar Illness?

The first concern for any parents when planning a family is for their infant to begin life healthy in mind and body. However, in spite of this desire, and even with the best care and planning, we cannot always plan for the difficulties that may arise regarding an infant's well-being when greeting the world. Couples in a bipolar relationship maintain this same intense desire but also need to know the additional risks related to having children and parenting.

As discussed in Chapter 1, research supports the theory of genetic predisposition to bipolar disorder, with a high probability that such inheritance involves multiple interacting genes. Many of these findings come from studies of twins and adoptions involving parents and children with this illness. These studies suggest that when one parent has bipolar illness, a 7.8 percent risk exists for a child to develop the disorder. When both parents have bipolar disorder, there is a 50 to 75 percent chance that their child will experience a mood disorder—either bipolar or another depressive disorder. However, we'll again emphasize that having a genetic predisposition does not always mean the bipolar symptoms will emerge.

As a couple you need to discuss your thoughts and feelings regarding these risks. Just as your shared knowledge and feelings regarding bipolar illness will support a rich and satisfactory relationship, reviewing these facts and voicing your mutual concerns will help you to arrive at the best decision for both of you.

Concerns for the Bipolar Mother

Women with bipolar disorder should be concerned about the impact of a pregnancy on their illness and the potential effects that their medications may have on the child. If your wife has bipolar disorder and you have decided to have a child, you should seek the collaborative counsel of a knowledgeable psychiatrist and obstetrician who will work as a team to offer you consultation throughout the pregnancy and beyond. Such planning and consultation can help both of you to manage the illness, minimize symptoms, and reduce potential risks to the fetus.

During the planning stages, identify a good support system for both you and your partner. This will be a challenging time and you need to be more keenly observant of any signs of the onset of an episode. Accordingly, you may want to obtain the help of another family member or friend with whom you are close, one who may have regular opportunities to observe your wife. Additionally, both of you may want to set up a support system to assist you after the delivery since it could be a stressful time as well.

Studies show that pregnancy and delivery often exacerbate symptoms of bipolar disorder. Specifically, according to the National Alliance on Mental Illness (*www.nami.org*), pregnant women or new mothers with bipolar illness have a sevenfold higher risk of hospital admission and a twofold higher risk for a recurrent episode, as compared to women with the illness who have had previous pregnancies. Additionally, women who discontinued bipolar medications between six months prior to conception and twelve weeks after conception were more than twice as likely to suffer a recurrence of at least one episode of the illness.

Hormonal changes during pregnancy are one factor that can contribute to a potential relapse. Specifically, it is hypothesized that an imbalance of hormones during this time can lead to mood changes by altering the brain chemistry. At the same time, physical discomfort, loss of sleep, changes in diet, and increased stress between you and your partner may further contribute to fostering an episode.

Lithium is the preferred medication for the treatment of bipolar disorder during pregnancy because when compared to Depakote, it has less potential risks for the developing fetus. However, due to lithium's side effects such as specific cardiovascular defects, hypothyroidism, and diabetes insipidus, first-generation antipsychotic medications may be recommended instead. If your wife decides to abruptly discontinue her medication upon learning of her pregnancy, be especially watchful for the symptoms of her disorder. Several studies suggest that relapse rates are greatest when a mother with bipolar illness quickly discontinues a mood disorder medication before or during pregnancy, rather than slowly withdrawing from it.

It is especially important that both you and your partner are alert to any symptoms that may occur during the postpartum period, which can be a traumatic time for any woman. This is when your wife may need the most support as she deals with new challenges relating to sleep, nutrition, social contacts, and the demands of an infant. Be alert to any symptoms of mania or depression during this time, as it is the period associated with high risk for symptom relapse or escalation. This is also the time when the stabilization of sleep patterns should be prioritized. Tranquilizer and sedative medications may be prescribed both during and after pregnancy to help regulate sleep.

It is common for new mothers to experience mild mood swings, sadness, anxiety, a diminished appetite, and difficulty sleeping as part of the "baby blues." Usually these symptoms disappear within a few days. By contrast, "postpartum depression" is more intense and pervasive and begins any time within the first year after childbirth. This condition is not limited to women with bipolar disorder. This form of depression may include thoughts of harming the baby, hurting herself, or feeling no interest in the newborn. In its most severe form it is referred to as "postpartum psychosis," a rare condition that includes visual hallucinations, delusions, cognitive confusion, and attempts to inflict harm on the baby or oneself. Careful monitoring by you and your support network is critical during this time.

Challenges of Pregnancy for the Nonbipolar Partner

Pregnancy accompanies a host of challenges that include the scheduling of medical consultations, maintaining nutrition, setting up space in your home, preparing for all of your infant's necessities, and taking care of your own general health. These demands can place an unusual burden on you as the mate of a bipolar partner. It requires the balancing of attention between your needs and those of your partner. It may also be a time when you allow yourself to get as much support as possible from friends and/or family, both during the pregnancy and following delivery.

The period during pregnancy and after delivery is a potentially stressful time for you, the nonbipolar partner. Your partner may feel ignored or displaced as your attention rightfully and increasingly focuses on your needs and those of your infant. This is the reaction of many men in such a situation, and it is a particularly stressful challenge for a man with bipolar illness. And, clearly, this can be an especially challenging time if you are a new mother having to also respond to difficulties that arise with your bipolar mate. Be as alert and attentive as you can to any signs of your partner's symptoms. Even more important, and in a proactive manner, emphasize an ongoing discussion with him from the moment you share your decision throughout every stage of pregnancy and delivery. Inquire about his concerns and reassure him that you will be there for him. In addition, discuss any plans to obtain support for the two of you.

As for any expectant couple, it will enrich your relationship to discuss your plans and hopes regarding your child and the family as a whole. Also, be certain to share the dreams you have as a couple, as parents, and as a family.

The Challenge of Parenting

New parents meet a fresh set of challenges, even when both partners are non-bipolar, but those in a bipolar relationship face a variety of unique demands. In general, while the bipolar parent may experience many new stressors, it is the parent without the disorder who may assume the lion's share of responsibility for the parenting. Although we are not suggesting that this be the case for all parenting tasks, we do want to underscore that you may be shouldering more of the burden than your partner. Therefore, be mindful of how you are parenting as a couple to ensure that your children experience the best possible parenting even though your partner lives with bipolar disorder.

Ideally, both partners should be equally involved in decision-making and the day-to-day tasks and rewards of being good parents to your children. If you are one of the fortunate people whose partner's illness is stabilized most of the time, the impact of her illness will be minimized. Whether your partner experiences few or frequent relapses, the attitude you convey regarding your bipolar partner—and how you treat him or her—will impact your parenting and the relationship your children develop with their bipolar parent.

It is strongly advised that you recognize your specific attitudes regarding bipolar illness and how your feelings influence how your respond to your partner. Be mindful that the views you maintain may be communicated to your children by words and actions. These key attitudes toward the illness and your partner deserve special attention and will be further addressed in the following discussions.

You Didn't Cause It

Human beings operate from both emotions and rational thought, no matter our age, education, or income level. Regardless of how often we hear something or grasp it intellectually, wishful thinking can be influenced by our emotions. Even though you are an intelligent and reasonable person who fully "knows" that you did not cause your loved one to be bipolar, your alter ego may still be saying, "Oh, but I know I did." Even if your loved one was diagnosed ten years before you met, you may still blame yourself.

Even if you understand that you did not cause the illness, you might still think that you're the cause of your loved one's manic or depressive episodes. This is simply not true. It can be difficult to identify specific triggers of an episode. The best you can do is be sensitive to what raises the stress level for your partner and do whatever possible to reduce it. While assuming the responsibility for your loved one's illness demonstrates your concern, the world keeps turning and you must live your own life too. You cannot completely shield your loved one from what is happening in the world, your life, or the life you, your partner, and your children share together.

To presume that you are the root of your partner's illness would indicate a grandiose notion of your emotional mind and may serve as a coping strategy to avoid recognizing and experiencing the real frustration of being unable to control the illness. Most significantly, behaving in ways that reflect this attitude will only cause your children to cultivate these same thoughts. If your children begin to feel responsible for your partner's illness, it places a burden on them and is equally unfair for your partner. While their childhood may suffer to some extent because their parent has bipolar disorder, such a burden can only lead them to have unrealistic expectations about responsibility, caretaking, and relationships in general.

What If My Partner Says It's My Fault?

All of us, at some point in our lives, have been accused of something that wasn't our fault. For example, a parent may have said, "See what you made me do?" when you innocently entered the room and startled them into dropping some object. Many of us are guilty of failing to accept responsibility for our own actions and have blamed others for our bad mood, headache, memory lapse, and so on. All too common is the tendency to blame some major life disappointment on someone else, for example: "If I never got married I would have been famous," or, "If I never listened to my father I would have gone to law school."

WORD TO THE WISE

Avoid Shame

Blaming others for our actions allows us to avoid the feeling of personal shame, that intensely uncomfortable emotion that encompasses the sense of inadequacy and not "measuring up." Self-disgust can lead to the humiliation of others.

If your bipolar loved one tries to blame some episode or some other unfortunate development on you, remember that wrongfully blaming problems on others is a common coping strategy. This does not imply that you should be someone's mental punching bag. Depending on the nature of your relationship you can agree to disagree, share your hurt feelings, dismiss the disagreement as a joke, or ignore it. Couples counseling can be useful, but if that's not a possibility you may want to try twelve-step groups like Al-Anon, where participants share their stories of coping with an ill loved one (specifically alcoholism, though many groups are open to all kinds of problems). You might also avail yourself of other support groups in your area that focus more directly on bipolar disorder or mental illness. You can find support groups in your area by contacting the Depressive and Bipolar Support Alliance (See Resources).

When your child overhears either parent blaming the other, he will be learning a negative message about how to be part of a relationship. Children want to please their parents. They also want to see their parents as competent and able to effectively manage their emotional life. Listening to messages of blame may lead children to feel overly responsible for the emotional well-being of a parent. While children may at times assume responsibility for a parent's mood, what they hear from you will reinforce their thinking.

No, You Cannot Make It Go Away

Since mental conditions such as bipolar illness sometimes manifest few visible signs of the disorder, people may believe that they can influence their bipolar loved one's thoughts or actions. Maintaining such expectations will only serve to exacerbate your annoyance with your partner and will make you more prone to act in ways that intensify his tension and frustration. When you behave in ways that reflect this type of distorted perception, you model unrealistic and problematic expectations that your children may internalize.

The attitudes you have toward bipolar disorder may underlie a specific pattern of interactions that you have with your partner.

Being mindful to avoid these behaviors can help improve your relationship as well as provide your children with a healthier respect for you and your partner. The roles you may find yourself playing include:

The Punisher

When children are punished, the punishment is intended to ensure that they never repeat the same mistake. Some people try these same techniques with their bipolar partners.

During moments of aggravation your emotions override your rational thought. They also fuel your belief that yelling loudly enough—or saying something cruel enough—will shock the bipolar disorder out of your partner. In addition to raising your voice, you may add a few insults in the hope that arousing shame will enhance your significant other's motivation for change: "You stupid so-and-so, do you see what you just did?" All that you will accomplish with such communications is instilling fear or resentment.

What is the potential impact of your attacks? Your children may learn that fear and degradation can be used as motivators to help them get what they want in a relationship. Or, they may internalize the need to be perfect in an effort to ensure that they will not be the target of such devaluation. Further, they may increasingly avoid being around you, since yelling is off-putting to everyone. Always remember that your behavior is held as a benchmark for your children.

No matter how frustrated you become, abuse will not help alleviate your partner's condition. In fact, studies have increasingly shown that communications that convey highly negative emotions have a detrimental impact on the course of bipolar illness. Additionally, children who observe verbal or physical abuse toward others are often just as seriously impacted as children who are the targets of such abuse.

The Prosecutor

We operate with an emotional brain and a rational brain. The prosecutor overemphasizes the rational to the exclusion of emotions and thinks that cold, hard evidence will convince the bipolar person that she is guilty as charged. The goal of the prosecutor is to help the other person recognize and agree with the "facts." The motivation in using this strategy is to help the bipolar partner gain clarity, as if enlisting her rational thought alone could override the chaotic mood shifts and impaired judgment that sometimes accompany bipolar disorder.

WORD TO THE WISE

Look Into Yourself

When you were a child, were you ever accused or punished for something you did not do? Did you think your own parents or caregivers really listened to your needs? Looking back, do you recall feeling responsible for a parent's moods? Did one or both of your parents have some serious mental condition or addiction? If you answered yes to any of these questions, unresolved feelings about your past may be contributing to the intensity of the frustration, hurt, or anger that you experience with your partner.

The hope is that this clarity will lead to a total reformation of character. For example, the prosecutor may confront the bipolar person with credit card bills acquired during a manic episode, or present her with a calendar with the carefully checked-off days it has been since the depressed individual has left the house. Maintaining such expectations reflects a denial of the reality of the disorder while also denying what your partner has to live with. Such denial will lead to her feeling further diminished and isolated.

These attitudes and behavior reflect a form of bullying and intimidation that will serve to confuse and create tensions for your children. While as parents you want to instill a sense of responsibility into your children, they need to know that bipolar illness can undermine responsibility and may, at times, lead to less than rational behavior. Also, while playing prosecutor may be an effective strategy in a courtroom, it is inhibiting and can even be experienced as abusive in a loving relationship. Such a role may force children to feel like they have to be overly attentive to justify their actions and emotions, a challenge that may lead them to become overly self-conscious, to a destructive extent.

Striving to Give Your Children Stable Childhoods

Whether your children inherit mood disorders or not, they will still be growing up with a bipolar parent and will come to realize that their parent has a serious medical condition. Your children need to be informed. It is more disturbing for a child to be given no explanation or to be told something that makes no sense, such as "Mommy just gets tired" or "Daddy's just having a bad day."

How a patient responds to treatment will figure significantly into how stable a parent he might be. The parent with steady moods who can function fully in society may still experience the usual ups and downs that parents go through when raising children. The parent who does not respond well to treatment is likely to be a less stable influence and may be incapable of teaching important life skills. Such inconsistency can negatively impact a child in a variety of ways. For example, a child may learn that people are not to be trusted or he may develop insecurity about his own self-worth. Some children may develop "pseudo-maturity," striving to act like an adult while renouncing or minimizing their age-appropriate needs for nurturance and support. This was the case for Adriana.

CASE STUDY: Adriana

Adriana, a twenty-nine-year-old woman, sought counseling to address her concerns about her choices when developing relationships with men. She indicated that all of the serious relationships she had developed in the last ten years were with men who were not fully emotionally available to her. This, however, was not her experience during the early days of their relationship. What went wrong?

When describing her family background, Adriana reported that her mother had bipolar disorder and that while her only sibling, a younger brother, suffered from depression she had neither mood disorder. Adriana indicated that her mother's illness was at times severe, requiring hospitalization, and that she had attained more stability at the onset of Adriana's teenage years. Throughout those earlier years her mother was ambivalent about her commitment to treatment and had difficulty finding the appropriate medication regimen. During Adriana's early development she experienced her mother as extremely unpredictable. Although she was usually a wonderful and loving parent who could be fully present and engaged while playing with Adriana, helping her with schoolwork, or discussing personal issues, at other times she appeared preoccupied and unavailable. Reflecting back, Adrianna realized that her mother's periods of preoccupation coincided with episodes of mania and depression.

While Adriana's father was present in her earlier life, he seemed less available as she approached adolescence. Earlier on, with a deep sense of love and concern, he had supported Adriana's mother and conveyed to his children the necessity of their being sensitive to the difficulties she experienced with relation to her illness. As time passed, however, Adriana recalled his increasing absence from home and how he was not fully "there" even when physically present.

Gradually Adriana began to worry about her parents' enduring love even though she still felt love from both of them. As the older child in the family, Adriana played a parenting role with her younger brother. She learned to understand her mother, and that awareness led to a degree of pseudo-maturity and intellectual understanding—but at the cost of ignoring the emotional needs appropriate for a girl her age.

The pattern of these early interactions led to Adrianna's absolute responsiveness when she met men who were emotionally open in the first stages of their relationships. Yet, these same men grew more distant and less dependable with time. Only later did Adriana realize how she had innocently gravitated toward men who, like her mother, were unpredictable in their availability. Adriana also learned that this was a protective coping strategy to help her deal with anticipated loss, a pre-emptive attempt to avoid pain. Likewise, she gained the understanding that what she had sought was a familiar type of relationship, which helped to trigger the difficulties with trust on which all early associations were based.

Sigmund Freud used the phrase "repetition compulsion" to describe a driving force in some relationships, which were characterized by unresolved issues. Like Adriana, we may inadvertently seek partners with traits similar to those with whom we experienced earlier conflicts. This might occur when, at some deeper level, we believe that correcting issues in a new relationship will help to resolve the conflicts of our past. Through counseling, Adriana learned to improve her ability to trust her own emotions while simultaneously being vigilant about healthy choices when seeking a partner.

Although your bipolar partner will still have an important relationship to your child, the child's experiences and attitudes toward his bipolar parent will be influenced by your view of bipolar disorder and how you relate to your partner. Your child, like yourself, will experience frustration and pain associated with his bipolar parent's illness since it is natural for a child to rely on a parent's unwavering dependability. How your child manages his reactions will also parallel how you manage yours and will strongly depend on your availability to talk about his feelings and reactions to living with a bipolar parent.

Your continued effort to maintain a good relationship with your mate conveys the idea that love transcends the illness. It also suggests that your partner, despite his illness, is able to meet many of your needs. Never lose sight of your child's vulnerability and always remember that the frustration you at times experience with your partner is magnified in your child, who is dependent on the stability of his parents. It's also important to remember that, just as your love for your partner goes beyond his illness, so does your child's. Even while there may be many frustrations and declarations of hurt or anger, know that such reactions are a natural part of even the healthiest of families.

ASK THE DOCTOR

How common is bipolar disorder?

It is estimated that 1 to 5 percent of the U. S. population is bipolar, which means that you might expect to encounter as many as 5 bipolar people for every 100 you meet. Therefore, it is increasingly likely that bipolar disorder will touch your life.

It's important for you as a parent to remember that your child's relationship with your bipolar partner is as meaningful to the child as the one she shares with you. You may be the one who earns the money, changes the diapers, bandages the cut knees, cooks the meals, buys the clothes, and drives the children to soccer practice. By contrast, your partner may stay home and watch television, be unable to work, and only sporadically engage with the children. Yet, the mystery of human relationships is such that one of the children in your household may grow up to prefer the company of your bipolar partner. Perhaps the child feels sorry for her, or maybe when lucid she is more fun, more interesting, or even demonstrates more understanding than you do. Also, maybe you get so carried away with shouldering the entire burden that you forget about crucial matters. To avoid this, make sure you are taking the following actions:

Let Your Children Know You Care

Don't assume that they know because of everything you are doing for them. Children need reassurance, especially when they observe that you sometimes falter under the heavy burden you shoulder. You cannot conceal your unhappiness, and if your children think of themselves as burdens they will harbor guilt ("I'm so much trouble"), resentfulness ("I didn't ask to be born"), or both.

Live in the Present

Children should never feel that their parents were happier without them. You may tell some funny stories about when you were a child or a teenager, but never imply that you wish you were back in high school before the bipolar problems existed. Maintain your focus on where you are today, which is the world that centers on your children. Being in the moment also means being present with their emotions and allowing them to share their feeling and concerns about living with a bipolar parent and life in general.

Let Love Trump Chaos

When people feel the burden of caring for another person, they might expect everyone and everything to be in perfect order. But when you are partnered with someone unstable, perfection is impossible, unless during a state of mania your partner cleans and organizes from top to bottom. So maybe you do not have the most "perfect" household on the block, dinner is sometimes late, and the living room needs straightening. But maybe yours is the most loving house on the block. Perhaps it was more important to hug your children and read them a bedtime story than to put away the grocery bags. Don't feel guilty about this!

Keep Things "Us" and Not "Me"

As much as possible, keep the bipolar parent involved even if she is heavily medicated and not fully present. Discuss things with your partner and, when she is relatively stable, give her the opportunity to make up for lost time by bonding with the children. Unless your partner is in no state of mind for company, schedule family dinners and quality time.

Give yourself this simple test: If your child were to say, "Mom/Dad, you're the greatest, too bad Dad/Mom is so useless," how might you feel? Would you gloat because you agree that your partner is an absentee parent? Or would you feel sad that your child has this perception and that your partner was not having a more positive impact on your child's life? Never gloat over your closeness with your child to the exclusion of the other parent; ultimately, you will pay a heavy cost. It is likely that sometime down the road your child will question your role in supporting this perception. He may also resent you for trying to keep him from having a strong relationship with his other parent. As in other families, it is important that each parent supports the child's love and respect for the other. Only then will you be viewed as "us" even when your partner is unable to be fully involved and present.

Love Is the Best Stabilizer

It is unhealthy for children to grow up without stability, not knowing what might reasonably be expected to happen next.

Stability is reflected in a parent's love and demeanor, and it is through such interactions that children internalize a view of the world as supportive and safe. A child also builds on a positive feeling of self-worth when she feels loved. This is especially crucial for children who are still in the process of forming their identities. Bipolar households are not necessarily less stable than other households, but the presence of this illness increases the possibility of crisis situations. If the bipolar parent needs hospitalization or is in a manic or depressive episode, it can be frightening to children and make them feel less secure. Even hypomania (mild mania) can take its toll, especially if the children feel they are not being heard and/or their parent never seems to remember anything they told her. At such moments children may be physically present yet feel emotionally abandoned and confused.

Although children cannot be protected from the inevitable tragedies of life, they can expect to feel parental love. Without this anchor other things will matter less. Someone who grew up without ever knowing her father may suffer the same issues as someone who knew her father but never felt his love.

When to Talk to Your Children about Bipolar Disorder

Some children pick up on things at a tender age. These children may hear the word *bipolar* for the first time and learn over time what it means even though they cannot, when reflecting back, pinpoint an exact time and place they made the connection. It would be nice if there were a magic age when a child is old enough to understand what makes Mommy or Daddy "that way." Unfortunately, however, theories vary as to when children develop cognitive skills and some seem more advanced at a certain ages than others.

Whether your child is informed at age four or age ten, he is still a child and is being asked to comprehend something that many adults cannot accept. Children need space to mature and should not be forced to prematurely grow up even though they cannot be protected from the challenges of a parent's erratic behavior. Their lack of maturity impedes their ability to understand and to be forgiving of someone who at times says and does things that are not rational. Facing the reality that a parent cannot fully control his behavior is a task that requires a kind of mental compromise associated with adulthood. Be sure to always inform a child in a manner that is age appropriate.

WORD TO THE WISE

Your Child Is Human, Too

Sometimes parents communicate to their children, either outright or subtly, that Mommy has her hands full taking care of Daddy's illness so they should please be extra-good and not make trouble. But children, like adults, are not perfect, and they have the same need as adults to vent their frustration.

Although some children might reflect back on their discovery as a positive experience, one of those moments when they experienced the transition from childhood to adulthood, other children might resent their stolen youth. It is important to respect a child's needs by permitting sufficient breathing room for him to grasp the situation without fear and confusion. Otherwise, a premature leap into adulthood may lead to a world of isolation, alienation, and a total disconnect with the child's own feelings.

It may be helpful for you and your partner to inform your child together, possibly in a professional setting with the presence of a compassionate doctor or therapist. Clarify for your child that his parent is not at fault, and that the illness does not take away from how much both parents love him. In a manner that is not overly simplistic or overly technical, adjust your conversation to your child's level of intellectual and emotional maturity. Your doctor's office or support group may have pamphlets for children that explain some of the more complex details in ways that children can understand, but let the first discussion originate from you and your partner rather than a pamphlet.

If your partner is hospitalized when your child needs an explanation, you may need to handle it yourself until your partner is feeling better and can be drawn into the conversation. Since a wealth of information is obtainable through the media and on the Internet, it is possible that your child has or will discover details about bipolar disorder on her own. Due to the amount of misinformation about bipolar disorder, not only is a discussion with your child important, but it is vital to clarify the truth. Your child may also have misinterpreted information that she learned elsewhere. Your youngster needs that human connection and you will also need to reinforce it with subsequent discussions, as it is impossible for your child to fully understand your partner's illness in one conversation. It will be an ongoing process, and the messages you provide to you children will continue to resonate through your words and body language.

Chapter 11
Responding to Your Partner's Episodes

The sooner you recognize and acknowledge that your partner is facing an impending episode the more responsive you will be in helping him effectively manage it. The more severe symptoms of bipolar disorder will immediately catch your attention. By contrast, those that are more mild in nature may go unnoticed, ignored, or even minimized. Always be alert to recognizing symptoms and be prepared for how best to respond when your partner is facing a bipolar episode.

What to Do for Your Partner

It may well be wise to err on the side of caution when your partner is facing an episode, be it mania, depression, or a mixed attack. Since the joy and fulfillment of your relationship is based on your partner's stability, it is understandable that you might at first deny, ignore, or minimize the presence of symptoms that could potentially threaten your sense of harmony. However, just because "she's been more manic in the past" or "he's depressed, but he says he's okay" does not mean you should rule out immediate professional help. It is better that your partner's doctor inform you that things are not so bad than to let a situation escalate to the point where it causes real harm.

WORD TO THE WISE

Keep Things in Perspective

You may view your partner's need for hospitalization as a personal failure or feel that he somehow let you down. Others who are involved in his hospitalization may convey a similar attitude. If and when this happens, your partner will internalize a sense of increased stigma and shame, and both of you will need reminding that hospitalization is a supportive and temporary resource to help manage a serious illness.

As you and your partner have developed certain dynamics in your relationship, you have formed basic patterns that determine how you relate and communicate with each other. These patterns may involve the sharing of activities, your chosen responsibilities for maintaining the home, and how assertive or directive you may be with each other. Keep in mind, however, that regardless of how you relate with each other during the more stable periods, the onset of an episode challenges you to act decisively and assertively in the best interest of your partner and your relationship. Inherently, you will need to trust and act upon your judgment, even when you feel disloyal or fearful of creating conflict between the two of you. While your loved one may initially be emotionally and rationally available to contribute to the decisions you make, the increasing severity of symptoms may force you to act independently of what your partner believes.

Strive to be loving and concerned yet sufficiently firm to clarify your needs and to assure they'll be carried out. Although your love for your partner is unconditional and it is not your intention to act against her wishes, you must take action when you deem it necessary. For example, you may feel the need to call the doctor for a quick consult about what to do or to facilitate hospitalization when indicated. Escorting your partner to the doctor or to the hospital can be handled relatively smoothly—even during an episode of rapid cycling—if your partner trusts you or trusts the process enough that she does not resist treatment and feels comfortable asking for help.

As the healthier partner in your relationship you need to guard against coming across as judgmental, anxiety ridden, or even angry. Since emotions can be contagious, the calmer you remain, the less you will be contributing to the feelings of shame, guilt, or anxiety that may encompass an episode or hospitalization for your partner. You may simultaneously feel sad for her and personally disappointed, and this admittedly is not the happiest moment of your life, but you have things under control, and they will get better again. Especially if it is not the first time your partner has required hospitalization, you need to convey this attitude even though you may experience moments of doubt.

If your partner does resist immediate treatment and an advance directive—a signed legal document in which your bipolar partner gives permission for another individual, such as a doctor or family member, to ensure that she receives proper treatment—is in place then someone has the legal authority to make sure your partner gets treatment. If your partner is resistant to help, the challenge may be too great to handle without assistance. In this situation you may need to call your partner's doctor, the hospital, or the police for added support. If no advance directive exists, and if your partner is insisting that "nothing is wrong," then you must be proactive about seeking the immediate help of the police and/or the family doctor. Depending on where you live, they may not have the legal authority to intervene, but that should not stop you from trying. In a crisis situation, you cannot act single-handedly.

If the police, the hospital, and your partner's doctor cannot intervene and your partner is resisting all help, you may want to contact a close friend or relative. You should enlist the help of a friend or relative who has a positive relationship with your partner, someone he is likely to listen to. Enlisting a friend's support should be based on the reality of that person's relationship with your partner and not just on wishful thinking that she could convince your significant other about his need for hospitalization.

If you have exhausted all possible options, you can still insist on certain limits and boundaries. Hopefully, you have already discussed with each other—and perhaps with a doctor—how to handle the symptoms of bipolar disorder and what is and is not "acceptable." While it may feel awkward, you may want to write up a contract that both of you sign. The contract should specifically state the kinds of behavior that will and will not be accepted without professional intervention. When specific in nature, written statements provide little room for confusion or misinterpretation of what will be expected. (If this seems demeaning to your partner, then also add some things that you will not do.) Such an arrangement/document may come in handy as a reference during a difficult time.

At times you may want to inform others of what is happening with your partner, whether by phone, e-mail, or text messaging, to advise them about what is going on and that you would appreciate emotional support. Informing others also serves to warn them about their own safety in the likelihood that your partner contacts them. If the situation involves physical violence, toward you or your children, you have grounds for calling the police. If your partner is dangerously aggressive, immediately get yourself or any other targets to safety. Call 911 or get to the police station.

Warning Signs of Suicide Risk

A part of being vigilant regarding your partner's well-being includes recognizing the signs that she may be suicidal. Some warning signs include:

- Expressions that life is too painful to continue living
- Constant worry, anxiety, and/or the inability to sit still
- Frequent and severe anxiety attacks
- A history of past suicide attempts
- Expressions of a suicidal plan
- Statements of the desire to die
- Comments that imply you will be better off if she were dead

Additional factors that increase the potential for suicidal behavior include a family history of suicide, a history of alcohol or substance abuse, and certain personality disorders.

ASK THE DOCTOR

What percentage of bipolar sufferers commit suicide soon after diagnosis?

Studies find that between 6 to 15 percent of people with bipolar disorder commit suicide early in the illness. The risk is much more severe during periods of intense depression or dysphoric mania—the form of bipolar illness in which mania and depression occur simultaneously or alternate frequently in a single day.

The most important and the most loving thing you can do for your partner is to help protect her from self-inflicted harm or from causing damage to others. Also, be mindful to neither blame nor place guilt on either your partner or yourself.

What to Do for Your Children

If at all possible, do not involve your young children in an intervention process. Even if they put up a brave front, it will be very unsettling for, say, a twelve year old—let alone a five year old—to act as "the parent" by forcing his mother into a car or holding his father's mouth open while shoving a pill down his throat. It is an excessive burden to ask a child to parent his parent, even if he expresses the desire. While your child will be forced to make some sense of your partner's bipolar illness, suggesting his active involvement in a crisis management situation is a responsibility to which your child should not be exposed.

This is not to advise that you go to the opposite extreme by pretending nothing has happened. Honor your children by replying to their questions, and let them express their sincere feelings. Avoid snapping at a child who appears confused about what is going on or for crying or getting angry when Mommy or Daddy acts like that. Your child's response is normal for her age level, and she is only being honest.

When caught up in the whirlwind of your own feelings and forced to focus on the tasks at hand, you may be less sensitive to how your children are being impacted and fail to attend to their needs. At such moments you may inadvertently stop them from feeling or expressing the same thoughts that you are also experiencing. Just as you cannot shout or cajole away your partner's bipolar condition, neither can you force your children to not experience what they are feeling. You may even need to force yourself to put your own feelings on hold to help them cope with the situation at hand. Remember that it is natural for a child to experience a variety of emotions when he witnesses his father carried away in an ambulance or learns that her mother has suffered a relapse and may be away for a month. While you will experience the pain of separation, a child is more vulnerable to the confusion and tension associated with such an event.

CASE STUDY: Reggie and Helen

Reggie was a wonderful father to his children, two boys with a three-year age difference. He was especially loving and protective with them when his wife, Helen, experienced relapses related to her bipolar disorder. Whether helping to prepare meals at night or providing lunches for the boys to take to school, Reggie was available. He made an effort to designate Sunday as sacrosanct, a "family only" day. On Sundays he took the children to a museum or to a sporting event, visited with relatives, or dined out with them—anything that would allow the entire family to spend some time together.

So it was not surprising that when Helen was too depressed or too manic to join the family on a Sunday outing, Reggie would ensure her safety before they embarked on their scheduled activity. Even when Helen's condition precluded their leaving the house, Reggie created interesting diversions that he shared with the boys at home. He equipped his basement with video games, board games, and physical fitness equipment and he taught them woodworking in the shop, which he set up in their garage. From designing a birdhouse to a go-cart, his sons were frequently the envy of their neighbors because of his handicraft. He also conveyed his caring through his capacity to openly share his feelings and be attentive to the feelings of his children. Reggie's single priority was in providing his children the best possible parenting. Whenever Helen was available, she was included as an integral part of the family cohesiveness.

When children are taught that their honest feelings (especially negative ones) are a nuisance to grownups, they grow to renounce their feelings and, in the process, lose touch with themselves. They may also feel shame and weakness when such feelings surface in their awareness. As a consequence, they grow to adulthood with the idea that they have no due claim to a full life and that if they act out or stand up for themselves they are "bad" and not worthy of the same rights as others.

WORD TO THE WISE

Have a Little Fun

Indulging your children as a means of making up for your partner's breakdowns and subsequent hospitalization is ill advised. But it may be the right time to offer some reasonable treat or enjoyable experience, like a trip to the movies, even a new piece of music, or a video game. Let them know that the entire world is not bleak, and reassure them of their right to enjoy themselves despite the difficult time their mother or father may be going through.

Some people make the mistake of thinking that children are too young to cope with such matters or that it's not important to talk with them or be comforting during difficult moments, particularly if the children seem fine. But, children are observant and at times see things more clearly than grownups. This stems from their lack of experience in avoiding uncomfortable feelings, which provides them with a finer vision than adults usually realize. Even if your child does not seem to understand, you still want to take the time to explain things to him.

Offer your children space to express their feelings, and be certain to convey yours in an appropriate manner. For example, it can be helpful and healing to say, "Yes, honey, I'm sad for Mommy, too." But it is inappropriate to say, "I'm really scared about what will happen to her!" or "I should divorce your mother; she's so impossible." It may also be wise to communicate these feelings in the presence of a therapist who can help guide the discussion in a positive direction.

Therapy may also be indicated if your child seems wounded by all that has happened. If the child is listless, cannot stop crying, does not want to play with other children, becomes increasingly aggressive or hostile with others, is doing poorly in school, has difficulty sleeping, or acts rebellious, then professional help is recommended.

Adult Children

If your children are grown and out of the house, are they available to help you during times of stress? The best way to find out is to inquire, as one adult to another. If your adult children want to be involved and have no serious problems of their own, sharing responsibilities can be a positive experience for the entire family. On the other hand, if they lack the patience required to effectively manage these situations, it is better they not be involved. Others may be too encumbered with their daily lives—job stress, family issues, or personal illness—to help out.

The child who harbors some deep-seated resentment toward you, her bipolar parent, or the very difficult circumstances surrounding her childhood may have little sympathy for the situation and opt to start distancing herself from the ongoing crises as soon as legally possible. Perhaps you or your bipolar partner acted unkindly or even ignored her during her childhood, or perhaps her feelings of helplessness or hurt experienced as a child are so strong that they resurface whenever her bipolar parent is present. Your child's reluctance to help may also be based on fears of her predisposition to bipolar disorder that are triggered by such visits. If you believe that emotional issues such as resentment are keeping your children at a distance, you may wish to discuss these concerns with them. But, it may be best to wait until after the crisis is resolved before you try to improve your relationship with your adult children in a meaningful way.

The unfortunate truth is that families find it easier to remain close when less turmoil is present. When parents are even-tempered, reasonable, and loving toward their children and each other, and if being at home with family is a joyful experience, the chance of the family growing apart is significantly less. It's also harder to expect family members to pitch in and help when the need for assistance is more frequently required. This is especially true if the problems were considerable when the children were growing up and they felt alienated from you, your partner, or each other.

Once the bipolar individual's symptoms are under control, your children should feel free to express their concern. Get-well cards or gifts may be appreciated, especially since your loved one has been sick, and the more you can normalize bipolar disorder as just another illness, the better. In a nonblaming way that does not make anyone feel guilty for what they did or did not do, the entire family can discuss the experience together. If necessary, have a professional present.

Be mindful that your adult children may have different perspectives from yours regarding your request for help. This may be due to their unique experiences growing up with a bipolar parent or unresolved sibling issues. Further, remember that you may waste precious time second-guessing their motives only to discover that their reasons have little to do with their parent's bipolar condition. When in doubt, ask and, based on their responses, determine if working toward improved family relations is a realistic goal. Remember, with adult children, you have limited influence.

What to Do for Yourself

You owe it to yourself to enjoy as full a life as possible. But, in the midst of a crisis involving a beloved partner, your own needs may have to be set aside until the emergency is over. For the next two, twelve, or forty-eight hours, you may not be able to think beyond your partner's immediate care.

If your partner is hospitalized, it's natural to find it difficult to go about your usual routine. The need to remain by your partner's side is very real. Although money may be tight and tensions high, try to do at least one nice thing for yourself. Do you enjoy long hot baths? Ice cream cones? Walking your dog in the park? Do you have a favorite CD to listen to? A support network is important during these trying times, and you should feel free to ask a close friend or family member to join you for coffee as a way of distracting you from the problems at hand, even if only for a few minutes at the end of the day.

It is when your partner has severe episodes or requires hospitalization that your strongest negative feelings will surface, and you may even have doubts about your relationship. Any lingering anger, frustration, anxiety, or sense of hopelessness that you may have been experiencing over time will precipitate self-doubt. Such moments may also underscore your sense of loneliness and your ambivalence regarding the continuation of your relationship, and you may begin pondering the advantages and disadvantages of ending it. However, this is not a constructive time to ask yourself such questions, because the turmoil you are enduring may override your capacity for clear and sound judgment. Do what you can to nurture yourself and shelve these problems for a time when you can think more logically and arrive at well-thought-out conclusions.

Responding to a bipolar episode will make demands on your time that may interfere with your work, your leisure time, or other relationships and activities that you enjoy. Although this is the time that your partner needs you the most, always remember to take care of yourself first. Being mindful of your own physical and mental well-being will also make you a better caretaker and parent to your children. The acknowledgment of your need for support during trying times is a major component to healthy living.

Chapter 12
What to Emphasize

Just as it is important to be mindful of situations and people you and your partner should avoid, you also should remain attentive to those people, activities, and attitudes that might help keep your lives happy and harmonious. Such consideration can help you through stable times and also the more difficult periods. In this chapter, we emphasize the need to find balance in daily life by just "being" as well as "doing" and learning to be mindful of what is really important in the big picture. We also emphasize the need for organization in terms of planning as well as creating a comfortable living environment and the importance of maintaining good health and open communication with your bipolar partner.

Neither Too Fast Nor Too Slow

It is almost impossible to not feel rushed in today's world. In fact, many of us seem to enjoy doing things as quickly as possible. Our emphasis on speed reflects our perceived urgency to achieve or produce as much as possible within a certain time frame. We focus our attention on doing, rather than being, since many experience achievement as the real measure of their self-worth. Ironically, the more gadgets invented to make our lives easier, the greater our expectations of what we believe we need to accomplish.

While this pressure may originate from others, oftentimes we inflict it both on ourselves and on other people. We frequently hear the word *multitasking*, doing two or more things simultaneously. At times, you cannot avoid multitasking: you may need to speak with a client while making dinner or assist your partner with her meds while helping your son with a math problem. Your partner may also have to multitask, but in a bipolar relationship, it may be smart to avoid multitasking when possible.

There is something to be said for doing one thing at a time and giving it your full attention. In doing so, you will be more present and engaged with whatever task you are addressing. While you cannot control another person and don't want to seem like a nag, gentle, loving reminders might encourage your partner to do the same. In trying to get your partner to reach a happy medium, you will also be helping yourself.

The following strategies identify some ways that you can help your partner achieve a balance between too fast and too slow:

- ***Differentiate between what requires immediate attention and what can be addressed at a later time.*** Think in terms of prioritizing the challenges of daily living. Sometimes people make huge deals out of small problems, and both you and your partner need to keep things in perspective. If a knob comes loose on the stove, the sky is not falling. Likewise, if something seems more challenging than your mate can handle, leave it for someone else. For example, if she is a nervous driver and a friend calls her for a ride to the airport, see if the friend can find someone else.

- ***Encourage your partner to seek help.*** Grandiosity, paranoia, the fast pace associated with mania, and the isolating aspects of depression may make it difficult for your partner to ask for help. Nevertheless, the sharing of responsibilities can help diminish stress.
- ***Encourage your partner to pace himself and take short breaks whenever possible.*** He can step outside for some fresh air, enjoy a snack, read a few more pages of a book, play a video game, listen to music, or even watch television. Other relaxation strategies that help calm the mind and body include the taking of deep breaths, exercise, yoga, and meditation.
- ***Avoid putting things off until the last minute.*** Encourage your partner to accomplish a small task each day to avoid rushing around at the last minute to meet a deadline.

Organization Can Be Less Stressful

Living with a bipolar person does not have to mean living with chaos or emphasizing fanatical control. You can find a middle ground. For example, work out a reasonable budget for what you can afford to spend on your home. Prioritize expenditures that reflect that budget, including attention to the essentials as well as leisure activities, entertainment, or special meals. With a small income, you can buy one DVD a month, or save to treat yourselves to that weekend getaway. Through banks and online services, you can even arrange to have your bills automatically paid each month. Or, you might be able to hire a reputable accountant to take care of your monthly expenses. In this way, you know where your money is going each month, but it's less accessible to your bipolar partner.

All too often, with the pressures of work and attending to chores, many of us put off finding time to relax. At times, we erroneously conclude that only a week-long vacation will provide us an escape from the pressures we face. By maintaining this belief we fail to recognize the many relaxing activities that require only a few hours of our time. Reading, engaging in a hobby, taking a bath while listening to music, playing a board game, or trying a new recipe are a few of the many activities that you and your partner can do to relax—either alone or together. Even if it means putting off mowing the lawn, make sure to give yourselves quality time together each week.

You can also find professional organizers—people who design, build, and/or buy the shelves, closet organizers, file cabinets, and drawers that you might use to develop easy ways of keeping things orderly and neat. By having outsiders help you organize your house, you will save hours of planning as well as implementing such plans.

Creating a Comfortable Home

Creating balance in your lives involves designing a comfortable and relaxing living environment, one conducive to enjoying the activities of daily living. To create this setting you must be attentive to every space in your home while identifying ways to help achieve your goals.

The General Home Setting

Maintaining a comfortable home environment is conducive to a more relaxed state of mind. By contrast, rooms full of clutter may only create further tension for your bipolar partner as well as for you. Any structure that is provided by routine, even in terms of consistently keeping the home in order, helps to maximize stabilization in dealing with bipolar disorder.

You don't need financial wealth to have a home environment that feels clean and comfortable. Even if money is tight, you can bring cheerful, colorful objects into the house. In recent years, the media has expanded on decorating ideas for those with a more modest budget. As indicated by do-it-yourself television shows, Internet websites, and interior design books and magazines, artistic talent is no longer a prerequisite for pleasing wall decorations. Sometimes a single addition of some interesting object can dramatically change the appearance of a room. You can find books at your public library that offer refurbishing ideas for a small investment.

Many benefits exist that follow the principles of feng shui in organizing your home, such as a clean and orderly residence. You are encouraged to keep clutter to a minimum while finding a place for everything. If possible, pay someone to help clean the house weekly.

When Dining

If you like to cook, keep in mind that smell and taste are related senses and that appealing fragrances might help to stimulate your bipolar partner's appetite during a time when she may not otherwise find food very tempting.

WORD TO THE WISE:
Ask Your Kids about Mealtime

Many children do not enjoy eating with the family, usually because they feel left out of the conversation. They're only asked about school, feel constantly criticized, or feel that they cannot relax and be themselves. When your children are antsy to be excused from the dinner table, ask yourself what is contributing to their desire for a quick departure. Are you unwittingly acting in a way to make them want to be excused? Are they experiencing discomfort at how their bipolar parent is behaving?

Similarly, some sources claim that warm colors such as red, orange, and yellow encourage eating. If there are no small children around to make doing so dangerous, go ahead and light candles. If you are religious, feel free to say "Grace." Anything that can make the mealtime seem like a wonderful event rather than a necessary chore—let alone an ordeal—can help. You may even want to select clothes beyond your casual outfits to help make a particular meal feel special.

A nicely set table and being fully present with each other, along with the food, can also stimulate a more intimate dining experience. Similarly, studies suggest that people are inclined to eat more and enjoy their food less when multitasking during a meal. Instead of watching television or reading the newspaper at breakfast, as many of us are guilty of doing, put on some soothing music instead. Attending solely to the food—and each other—will promote your shared pleasure and overall calmness.

Yet at the same time, do not get carried away. Especially with children at the table, mealtime is unlikely to be an oasis of tranquility. There may be table manners to correct, fights to be broken up, spills to be cleaned, and so forth.

The Bedroom

The setting of a room, including the colors chosen for the walls and the arrangement of furnishings, can all have a significant impact on the mood of both you and your bipolar partner. It is especially important to remember this when setting up your bedroom.

The bedroom should also be a cheerful place, and, contrary to the kitchen/dining area, cool colors like green, blue, or violet help induce calm and sleep. Comfortable, soft bed linens do the same. They may cost a little more, but since we spend an average of one-third of our life sleeping, it's worth it to make sure it's a pleasurable experience. This ideology should also extend to the bed, which should have a mattress that suits your preferences for comfort.

Keep the bedroom as dark as possible. This may require that you turn around clocks that give off light and unplug other electronic devices that emit some light even when shut off. If you fall asleep with the television on, make sure you set the sleep timer. Or perhaps doze off to soothing music. If you are religious or spiritual, perhaps pray together before going to sleep. And, of course, let us not forget the possibility of making love. In keeping with enhancing the atmosphere for physical intimacy, it is best to avoid having arguments in the bedroom or in bed. Doing so creates tension that can often become associated with the room as well as with falling asleep and physical intimacy.

Try not to bring anything work-related into the room with you. Keeping the bedroom uncluttered helps to create a relaxing environment conducive to sleep. And remember, the only thing more disheartening than falling asleep in a messy room is waking up in one.

Staying Healthy

While staying healthy is a goal that everyone can embrace, specific issues regarding bipolar disorder need to be addressed. Keep in mind that staying healthy is especially important for your bipolar partner, as this illness can cause him to be vulnerable to negative reactions to even slight changes in routine, including sleep or eating habits. Additionally, staying in good health is also related to maintaining a stable and positive mood. Clearly, this is just as important for you as it is for your partner.

Healthy Sleeping

Given the manic tendency to stay awake and the fact that some medications can be associated with insomnia, healthy sleep is especially important. Neither can you be expected to carry your share of the weight if your partner keeps you up all night.

What you and your partner need to do is find out what works best to ensure that both of you get a good night's rest. If you can sleep comfortably in one bed, so much the better, but if separate beds or even separate bedrooms are needed, then so be it. You can always periodically "raid" your partner's bed space to keep the passion alive. However, if your partner sleeps in a different room, try to make sure that nothing in the space could be harmful—including pills. Also, make certain there is nothing in the room that could overexcite your partner and cause insomnia. Remember, beyond a certain point your partner, as an adult, cannot be managed in the same way you would control a child. Yet, in a helpful and loving way you could say, "Are you sure you want to read that murder mystery in bed? It might keep you awake."

Exercise

We all know it is good for people to get fresh air and move around and that many people will go out of their way to drive even the shortest distance rather than walking. It also is commonly known that it is better to be fit and trim than overweight or obese. Your bipolar partner may tend to be either lethargic, seldom doing much of anything, or overly active and in need of slowing down.

Balance is the key. Working out in a gym is excellent, but be mindful if your partner is turning into an "exercise addict." If exercise is the only subject on her mind, and if she becomes agitated over having to miss a single day in the gym, there may be deeper issues going on.

Unless there is some prohibitive physical disability involved, you do not want your partner to become immobile. Do not wait on your partner hand and foot, but let him run some errands to get out of the house. If you are already in the kitchen when your partner calls out for a glass of juice, it is common courtesy to get it for him. But if he always calls out for you to get him something to eat or drink, regardless of where you are or what you are doing, you have a problem.

Working out together or jogging around the block are excellent shared activities that allow both of you to stay in shape while having fun together. You also can make sure that your partner neither overdoes it nor stops exercising altogether. If you can afford it, hire a professional trainer to help your partner implement a well-balanced exercise regime.

Healthy Eating

You don't have to be a "health food nut" to be vigilant about your partner becoming a "junk food junkie." Subsisting on candy bars or chips can throw anyone off balance, and that includes you. If possible, consult a dietician for the best kind of foods for both you and your partner, since your health is just as important. You might also involve your partner in meal planning to help ensure that he eats normally. However, if your partner is highly depressed and so not eating at all, remember that eating something is better than nothing.

Maintaining a Social Life

It is a good idea not to permit your life to revolve totally around your partner, and the reverse is also true. Part of creating balance includes the ability to maintain social relationships with others; it is important to have other people in your lives. Even if your partner is heavily medicated, at least some interactions with other people is advised—that is, unless it is unsafe for some reason. Getting together with family members or close friends can provide a healthy, nurturing atmosphere. Support groups can also be valuable assets.

While the active presence of others can help ease life's burdens, social outlets can also help your partner maintain ties while learning to get along with other people. Invite friends over for food or games and attend social gatherings as a couple. Even small things, like remembering how to converse without monopolizing a conversation, can be learned from such get-togethers. Games often require cooperation, as do mild tasks like setting up a summer barbeque. If you need help with major tasks, try to make them fun, like a paint-the-living-room party for which you provide the pizza. You might also consider small group activities that help other individuals. For example, perhaps your local park is having a tree planting party, or maybe you and your family can volunteer to stuff envelopes for a cause you all agree is worthy.

WORD TO THE WISE:
Empower Your Partner

Your partner may, at times, be inclined to educate others regarding her bipolar condition. This can be a challenging burden, especially if she is in an unstable period, has internalized a lot of stigma, or feels the need to justify her use of medications. However, if she has accepted her illness, then advocating the education of others could heighten her sense of empowerment.

Remember, the value of enjoying life as a family is the ability to engage with each other in rewarding and pleasant activities. If your partner has episodes, you might want to plan around them. Especially if the episodes are cyclical, you can plan activities for when your partner is likely to be the most cogent. You also can avoid activities that frustrate your partner or bring out his manic tendencies. For example, some people are poor sports about losing board games, and newer computer games can produce obsessive reactions. If your partner is highly medicated, it is best not to let him engage in responsibilities that might risk the lives of your children, like boating or building a fire.

It is important that both you and your partner seek out relationships with people who model behaviors or attitudes that can positively influence your partner.

These kinds of people include:

- ***People who lead balanced lives:*** These are people who eat three square meals a day, get a good night's sleep, fulfill their daily responsibilities, make time for leisure activities, and reflect constructive habits in managing finances. The benefit of forming such connections is that we can foster in ourselves the same goals as those held by the people with whom we share time.
- ***People who treat your partner like an equal:*** Someone who has no interest in "fixing" your partner, but is looking for genuine friendship and is willing to tell it like it is, may be a good person to have around.
- ***People whose company is enjoyable:*** This may seem obvious, but nobody wants to socialize with people whom they do not enjoy. It's important for your bipolar partner to be in the company of people who inspire him with a happy and positive outlook of life.
- ***People who solve their problems:*** Everyone has problems and things that go wrong, but healthy people work on resolving their difficulties and move on. They let go of those things they cannot control. They are not "addicted" to chaos and complications, but are people who are fun to know because they will not burden you or your partner with their own personal problems.

Learn What Works—and Do It

Effectively addressing the special needs of living with a bipolar partner depends to a great extent on identifying strategies that work and being mindful to practice them. Such attentiveness involves the monitoring of personal attitudes and behaviors that together have a positive impact on your partner and on your relationship as a whole.

Being Flexible

It is understandable in any relationship to have expectations for how a partner "should" behave. But, the success of the relationship depends on our capacity to be flexible in our expectations. We can hope or wish that a partner be a certain way, but rigidly holding on to such prospects may lead to individual suffering and tension within the relationship—especially with a bipolar partner.

Flexibility is essential when assuming control in your relationship and means that you accept your loved one the way she is rather than hoping she might change her ways and alter her behavior. Your ability to manage your disappointment is key to many of life's frustrations, even while you simultaneously hope that your partner meet the important expectations and core values on which your relationship is based.

WORD TO THE WISE

Put Emotional Needs First

People sometimes think the most important priority is maintaining rules when emotional needs should come before any rigid adherence to maintaining order.

Remember, everyone has personality defects, but when partnered with a bipolar person—particularly one whose treatment is only partially effective—it is easy to get caught in the trap of viewing yourself as "the healthy one." Be aware of any tendency you may have for "all or nothing" or "black-and-white" thinking. For example, even though you need to sometimes take charge, do not assume you need to take over every aspect of your relationship.

Similarly, just because your partner may be needy at one moment does not imply that she cannot take charge and be available to address your needs. Although you may need to set limits, make decisions, and balance the checkbook, it doesn't mean that your judgment is always correct, even though you are not the one who is chronically manic or depressed. Be aware of the rigid thinking that predisposes you to believe you are "right" and your partner is "wrong." The two of you, like everyone else, have differences in beliefs, behaviors, and in how you emotionally react to a particular situation. Remember, we all, at one time or another, have difficulty owning up to a mistake or letting go of a plan that did not work; this tendency is exacerbated if we've also been placed on a pedestal.

Flexible thinking helps to develop more realistic expectations regarding you and your partner. Therefore, if he will only eat his vegetables if he has dessert first, then so be it. It may be unusual, not the way you were raised, or not what you had in mind, but if he likes spaghetti for breakfast and oatmeal for dinner, respect his preference. At least he's eating. If you would like him to work full time and he is only working part time, focus on the positive contribution that he is making.

Keep a Journal

Since the human memory is imperfect, nobody can be expected to recall every little thing that happens. On occasion, we completely forget something or may even have faulty recollections of what really occurred. Journaling helps you, your partner, and your relationship by offering you the opportunity to jot down and express your feelings. It also helps to heighten your awareness regarding your emotions and thoughts.

Note-taking about a specific interaction with your partner may give you insight about a similar situation in the future. Such monitoring can be helpful in identifying alternative ways of handling a situation in a more constructive way. Reflection supported by journaling provides direction for improvement in any relationship, but it can be especially effective when you're living with a bipolar partner.

Journaling can also provide you a log of your partner's behaviors and moods at certain times of the day, week, or year. You can keep track of conversations with the doctor and suggestions from your support group. If or when a major episode strikes, it's remarkable how easily you can be caught off guard. Looking into the past for possible answers may prove worthwhile. Journaling may also be useful to the doctor—or even your partner—provided he is open-minded about receiving input. If you do keep a journal, make sure it is safeguarded in a private place so you can jot down strong language to get it off your chest without your children or partner seeing what you wrote.

Be Honest and Open to Criticism

It is important that you don't assume something has worked out well just because you haven't heard anything to the contrary. For example, if you have children, do not assume they are "fine" just because they answer affirmatively when you inquire. Even small children may be sensitive and not want to hurt your feelings, or they may lack the vocabulary or maturity to do anything but agree. Children can be highly sensitive to their parents' pain and behave in ways to reduce it, even at the expense of revealing personal feelings.

There can be a universe of difference between asking someone, "Are you okay?" or "Are you happy?" and "How are you?" The former frequently is a cue that the "correct" answer is *yes*. Asking your partner or your child "Is everything okay?" can be interpreted: "I want you to be okay because I don't want to have to do anything more for you, nor do I want to burden my mind with worry over you." On the other hand, asking "How are you?" provides an open-ended inquiry that is more likely to grant you an honest response.

Even then, some may respond by saying that they are fine when they are not, but it paves the way for a more straightforward reply, such as "I feel lousy."

To get beyond the "okay syndrome," you must be willing to hear that things are not okay and to present yourself as the strong, open-minded person who only wants the truth. You similarly need to reassure others of your ability to handle the truth, since actions speak louder than words. Your partner and children may be fearful of hurting your feelings and worry that you might explode in rage or break their hearts by crying.

WORD TO THE WISE

Use Others as Mirrors

A cliché that often rings true states, "If you don't like something about another person, it means you don't like it in yourself." When your children complain about some fear or disorder in their lives and you get angry with them, they might really be voicing what you are afraid to admit to yourself.

How do you know if they feel this way about you? If they never tell you anything but that things are "okay," this is your first clue. It is also helpful to let down your guard. Although many burdens may fall to you, you and your partner are in this together. It is possible to be viewed as worthy of respect while still admitting to the existence of a problem. If your partner says, "I had to wait forty-five minutes for my prescriptions to be processed," in a knee-jerk attempt to reduce frustration you may say nothing. Or, worse yet, you may say something to maximize her discontent. Preferable would be to respond empathically: "I hate when that happens. Just the other day it took me a half-hour to get out of the parking lot at the mall." If your seven-year-old daughter says, "It scares me when Mommy gets angry," rather than reply, "Never talk about your mother that way," you might instead be candid in your reply: "I know. It scares me, too, sweetie, but we all have to remember that Mommy gets sick sometimes and she doesn't mean it."

CASE STUDY: Wayne and Britney

Whether being flexible about new ideas, maintaining a journal, or remaining open to criticism, an effective strategy for identifying what works for you is to set aside time on a weekly basis for open discussion with your mate. Wayne and his wife, Britney, who lives with bipolar disorder, committed to practicing this approach several years ago. "At first it felt awkward," said Wayne. "For years I've held weekly meetings at the office to discuss and highlight specific strategies, which have proven successful in meeting the challenges of our work. Since these sessions offer the opportunity to share different opinions while improving our communication and trust, I decided it could also work at home."

Britney says, "Initially, when Wayne first broached the subject, I was concerned about his using these discussions to vent his frustration and criticize me—especially with regard to my bipolar illness. Instead, these discussions have evolved into a wonderful and intimate time spent together. Although we review any conflicts that may have arisen during the week, our focus is on how we dealt with these issues and how we may improve our method in the future. The result is a deepening understanding and appreciation of Wayne, while he has become more in tune with my concerns. Our mutual sharing has heightened our responsiveness to each other and the challenges we face by living with bipolar disorder. Additionally, Wayne has learned to provide me with positive feedback, rather than criticism, which I accept as gentle reminders of how to take better care of myself."

To summarize, if you find it wearisome to feel responsible for reducing or removing all of your family's pain, remember that compassion—both for others and for yourself—recognizes that we are human and that being human involves suffering. Even though we may wish for perfection, we can only strive to do our best.

Chapter 13
Putting Yourself First

Throughout this book we have emphasized the need to take good care of yourself, for you, your partner, and for your relationship. A part of care entails finding ways to feel empowered, identifying what you can do to feel hopeful and powerful, rather than powerless, and recognizing the choices and actions you can take to increase control in your life. In an effort to further enhance such empowerment, this chapter offers strategies that can impact you at a deeply personal level and that can have a far-reaching significance.

Remembering Self-Compassion

Self-compassion involves being sensitive to your own suffering, just as being compassionate involves sensitivity to the hardships of others. Similarly, just as compassion pushes you to act in ways to lessen your partner's suffering, self-compassion involves taking action to diminish your pain.

Being self-compassionate in your relationship involves recognizing and accepting both the positive and negative feelings you may have with regard to living with your partner. While you may do so at times, the more you deny, ignore, or minimize your negative feelings, the more you will experience resentment and act out these feelings. When you harbor negative feelings you can still maintain an orderly home, know your partner's prescriptions by heart, and even make sure a single check never bounces. However, your failure to recognize your own suffering may lead you to respond to your partner's needs in a cold, begrudging way, which makes life harder both for you and those you live with.

When you harbor a lot of resentment, anger, or hatred toward another person, it takes its toll on your psychological, emotional, and physical well-being. You may present a smile to the world, but underneath the façade you are steaming with negativity. If you are obsessing about what your partner did or did not do, how much you wish this bipolar thing would just disappear, or how much better your life would be without your bipolar mate, your energy is being sapped by your obsessions. You may have difficulty concentrating or finishing projects that would mean a lot to you. Perhaps such obsessing is causing you to self-medicate through the abuse of alcohol or drugs. Or, maybe you are not eating or sleeping very much and putting yourself at risk for cardiac problems related to tension.

Being self-compassionate means recognizing your emotions and doing something to address them so not to constantly carry such resentment. It also means arriving at a decision, a resolution to accept the facts of your situation and your relationship. You need to fully accept that your partner has a chronic illness and that it can flare up at times and be disruptive to both of your lives. Acceptance can mean being mindful to all that you love about your partner even, and perhaps most significantly, during those times when the illness seems to take over and mask what you truly love most. Conversely, full acceptance of your feelings may also lead you to end the relationship. In either case, it is self-compassion that will help free you from useless obsession and resentment.

Resentment, tension, and frustration often arise when we compare how life really is and how we imagine it "should" be. These negative feelings are often a distraction from the mourning and grieving process that is necessary to fully accept what we cannot control. Hoping and imagining your partner freed from the affects of bipolar illness may at times help to curtail your suffering, but you need to recognize what you can and cannot control and know the difference between the two. Such acceptance takes time and is based on an ongoing commitment that must be adhered to even when experiencing despairing moments.

CASE STUDY: Catherine and Peter

Catherine had been introduced to Peter through a mutual friend and was immediately attracted to everything about him. Although her friend informed her about Peter's bipolar condition, she convinced herself they would make a wonderful couple. Right from their first meeting Peter seemed fully present with Catherine, and they formed a powerful emotional connection. His zest for life was reflected in every aspect of his being, from the enthusiasm he expressed about his vocation as a college instructor to his joy in traveling to his passion for writing fiction. In everything they discussed, Peter expressed himself with excitement and a keen curiosity about life.

Nevertheless, it was early on that Catherine faced the first challenge that threatened to disrupt their relationship. Although Peter had been stable during the early months of their relationship, he began to exhibit the first symptoms of mania. The warning signs were triggered by events surrounding a trip abroad to research material for a new writing project, the pressure of deadlines regarding teaching assignments, and changes in his work schedule. All these circumstances began to impact his sleep and even the consistency with which he managed his medications. But, as he rapidly stabilized Catherine reassured herself that such episodes could easily be managed.

She and Peter continued to date, soon became engaged, and were married one year to the date after their first rendezvous. Some months later, Peter experienced the alternation of moods, beginning with mania and culminating with severe depression. The death of his mother, a severe case of flu, and the publication of his second book—although a positive event—combined to exacerbate his bipolar condition. While Catherine felt challenged by Peter's previous manic episodes, she was more impacted by the intensity of his depression and felt completely helpless and hopeless. His depression also triggered her feeling of abandonment.

During the next two years, Catherine and Peter struggled with the challenges of living a bipolar relationship. As she grappled with anger and frustration, she felt motivated to do whatever possible to help Peter and to preserve their marriage. Even when Catherine experienced the most intense self-doubt, she acknowledged that life with Peter was so fulfilling that she was committed to make the relationship work. Through self-compassion Catherine researched the illness to learn everything she could about Peter's bipolar condition. Gradually, she became pragmatic about what she could do to help Peter and what was beyond her control. This quest for information and strategy included educating herself about all available approaches, many of which are presented in this chapter.

There are many ways to practice and embrace self-compassion. These include:

- ***Self-help support groups:*** Bipolar support groups are available in most areas of the country to provide you and your partner with information and help. Some have sessions designed exclusively to meet the needs of caretakers. The group shares specific strategies to help alleviate the pain of living with this illness and can also provide you with a good reality check as to what you can realistically expect of yourself and your partner. Participation will help you to feel less alone in dealing with your unique challenges.
- ***Education:*** Reading self-help books like this one can provide valuable information and specific strategies to reduce the stress of loving someone with bipolar illness. Books dealing with negative emotions—shame, anger, anxiety, guilt, and depression—can provide you increased self-awareness and the necessary skills to effectively manage your negative emotions. DVDs and articles available on the Internet similarly offer information to enhance self-compassion.
- ***Stress management:*** Stress takes many forms. It may consist of emotional and physical symptoms that lead to more serious forms of physical illness. By studying time management (regarding work, home, and leisure time), organizational skills, relaxation exercises, and assertiveness skills you can practice self-compassion and reduce your stress. Physical exercise and related activities such as yoga and meditation can also help decrease stress's negative impact.
- ***Psychotherapy:*** Psychotherapy offers a safe haven to increase self-awareness and specific skills for reducing personal suffering. In the context of individual psychotherapy you are guided to more effectively manage your suffering while working on a more satisfying way of life for you as an individual

> and as a partner in your relationship. Psychotherapy can provide insight into how your personal habits and expectations of a loving relationship may both contribute to or reduce individual and shared satisfaction.

As we have emphasized throughout this book, couples psychotherapy is a valuable means of achieving greater self-compassion and compassion as you each address the unique challenges you face together. Through the guidance of a mental health professional you can learn to better understand and communicate with each other while recognizing your individual differences and how to address them. Couples therapy also provides increased understanding and strategies for partners who find the need to end an unhealthy relationship that can no longer be saved.

The selection of a psychotherapist should be made very carefully since you (or both of you) must feel comfortable sharing the most intimate details of your life with your psychotherapist. You may need to interview several therapists before selecting the one you feel is the best fit. Remember, therapy may at times be painful, but you need to process your pain before you can heal and achieve a more satisfying life.

Making Time for Yourself

It may sometimes be difficult to find quality time for yourself when in a bipolar relationship. While this challenge may not be as great when your partner is stable, the task of helping her remain that way can be demanding of your time. With this in mind, it is essential that you take time for yourself.

Getting Organized

Becoming organized may require some careful planning, whether you write down a schedule or create one electronically. The few moments it takes to organize your day by jotting down appointments and tasks can make a world of difference and save you time in the long run. You will also experience less tension in general.

A part of such planning involves prioritizing what needs to be done. This can be helpful for your whole family. We all get overwhelmed with too much on our plate, and the feeling of being snowed under makes us vulnerable to irritability and resentment, neither of which is good for you or those you love.

Leisure Time

All too often—and especially in recent years—the pressures of our daily lives force many of us to deny ourselves time for some form of leisure activity. Too many people believe they can only relax on vacation. This attitude fails to take into consideration the little time needed for leisure activity compared with the nurturing and energizing benefits derived. Today, many people settle for relaxing in front of the television rather than engaging in an activity that may lead to greater gratification, such as participating in a favorite hobby, reading a good book, listening to music, visiting with a friend, or selectively viewing the kind of movies you most enjoy. Being mindful of how you spend your leisure time will provide increased happiness and the strength to face the more challenging tasks of your day.

Recognizing and Overcoming Challenges

Be wary of any feelings that may interfere with your ability to set aside relaxation time for yourself. For example, you may so strongly embrace the identity of caretaker that you prioritize the needs of your partner and children to the exclusion of your own. If you are one of those individuals who rely solely on the role of caretaker as a way of experiencing positive self-worth, you may be denying yourself the ability to explore and expand your sense of self. Although caring for your partner is a noble responsibility, self-care is essential to your well-being.

You may also see yourself as someone who must constantly achieve and produce—at the expense of living in the moment. This trait, most frequently associated with "type A" personalities, is indicative of overly valuing these activities as a measure of self-worth. You may have lacked adult models who conveyed the importance of relaxation and play as an integral part of a full and meaningful life. You may even have become so competitive that you're afraid of falling behind should you pause to refresh. This belief can place unnecessary stress and tension on your relationship, especially if your partner is bipolar. You will also be less productive.

ASK THE DOCTOR:
What is the difference between "pleasure" and "gratification"?

Martin Seligman, a psychologist who has studied happiness, distinguishes between activities that provide "pleasure" and those that evoke "gratification." He believes activities that arouse pleasure are short-lived but memorable, such as enjoying a good meal, watching a movie, or reading an interesting novel. By contrast, those that offer gratification lead us to expand our identities and enrich our sense of competency, thereby offering more lasting happiness. This includes developing skills like painting, drawing, woodworking, growing plants, and photography.

Effectively managing these tendencies involves the need for increased vigilance in monitoring your emotions and behaviors. Finding new ways to reduce tension while practicing self-compassion will allow you to value yourself in ways that extend beyond competitive behavior or being a caretaker.

Remember the Big Picture

At one time or another we all are guilty of making a proverbial mountain out of a molehill, treating something trivial as though the fate of the world depended on it. To guard against this happening, try to keep the problems of everyday life in perspective. Was it really a calamity that you had to wait a long time in the grocery checkout line? Was it that important that your partner forgot for the tenth time to put the meatloaf in the oven?

By increasing your sense of purpose in life, you will not be unreasonably stressed out when issues like this occur. Only with a strong connection to yourself—knowing who you are, what you want to accomplish, what you most value, and what you need to do to accomplish your mission—can you achieve a greater sense of purpose. Your goal may have nothing to do with wealth and fame, but rather could be something as seemingly simple as wanting to be a good parent and a good partner. Keep in mind that any frustration or resentment may be directly related to painful experiences that you're suppressing rather than some recent and relatively minor event. If perfectionism is your problem, this leads to unrealistic expectations of your partner, yourself, and the world in general. Remember, when you can free yourself from obsessing on trivial things, you will be amazed at how much more energy and time you will have to devote to other, more productive endeavors.

Worrying Is Not Magic

If your partner experiences frequent bouts of instability, it is only natural that you will worry—about your partner, your relationship, your children, the bills . . . the list of things you can worry about is endless. However, while it is perfectly normal to worry, it's important to avoid falling into the trap of worrying excessively. Remember, worrying will not change anything.

There is a difference between understandable worry and excessive worry. Excessive worry is rumination, dwelling on, and repeating thoughts with no constructive purpose. They drain energy and the ability to take action. Some people can waste an entire day, week, month, or even a full year doing nothing but obsessing about everything wrong in their lives. This is wasteful energy, especially when obsessing about other people, because, as hard as it is to change yourself, you cannot change others. But, when your mental energy is focused on concerns other than problems, you may find more time for other things. For example, if your partner is frequently unstable and has been hospitalized, you might use this time for activities you would like to do. Take the time to catch up on things you have been meaning to attend to, or do something that is personally enjoyable.

Excessive worry may arise for a number of reasons. For example, it may be your disposition to expect the worst or a basic insecurity about always wanting to know "what comes next." Excessive worry may also derive from you feeling responsible for your partner, an overriding sense of blame that you somehow should be doing something more to shield him from pain. Such worrying may derive from shame, a global and negative self-evaluation that interferes with your personal enjoyment when your partner is suffering

At times, rumination can be a distraction from taking action that might be anxiety arousing. For example, you may spend hours dwelling on your resentment over situations regarding your partner or fantasizing how things could be. You may even blame her for not applying for a new job, going back to school, getting a promotion, or even taking the time to pursue her passion for photography. By worrying about your partner, you may be distracting yourself from acknowledging your own anxieties about pursuing your dreams. Such thoughts may also keep you from addressing ambivalent feelings about your relationship and its uncertain future.

Dealing with the Past and Forgiving Yourself

Just as your partner may harbor remorse over things he said or did in the past, so may you. Some of your regrets may be related to how you treated your partner, but they may also include how you treated your children, relatives, friends, coworkers, or even your letter carrier. Learning how to manage these regrets through forgiveness is an essential step in dealing with your past.

Being human means that we inherently make mistakes. By rigidly clinging to expectations of perfection, or thinking that you must always be right, you remain engaged in a futile effort to overcome this fact of life. You are also setting yourself up to feel resentment and annoyance with others and with yourself. Instead of recognizing and acknowledging your disappointment and shame regarding your failure to live up to your expectations, you may find it easier to resent others.

By contrast, forgiving yourself is part of the process of letting go of the past, an example of self-compassion. One constructive approach is to explore the behaviors you regret in an effort to "explain" what led to them rather than focus your energies on "blaming" yourself. Looking for an explanation for your behavior leads to a real understanding that may help you identify how you can act differently in the future. And while some blame can motivate you to improve your behavior, too much can foster a self-devaluing toxic guilt that inhibits objective self-examination and real change.

If you feel it important to explain yourself—or even apologize—to the people you may have treated poorly, then do it for yourself. But you should not expect or demand that they forgive you. There is a big difference between saying "I am sorry" and saying "Forgive me." "I'm sorry" expresses how you feel, and then you release control of the situation, whereas with "forgive me" you are still trying to control what another person should do. Remember, when people feel that an apology is too little, too late, they are too hurt to forgive. Others may be vindictive and small-minded. But in either case, you have no control over other people.

Loving Nonbipolar People

Sometimes new mothers spend so much time around their infants that they start talking to everyone in baby language. Likewise, you may spend so much time with or worrying about your bipolar partner that you forget what it is like to be around a person without a bipolar disorder. Several problems may arise here.

One outcome of living with a bipolar partner may be that you have little desire to be with others. This may be true if you do not experience relationships with others as reciprocal and supportive. Perhaps, because you are overwhelmed, you instead experience them as overly needy. In this case, rather than withdraw you may decide to spend time identifying your needs and voicing your concerns. You may also need to seek the company of those who seem more likely to reciprocate. You may also ask yourself if you seek friends who are needy or whose lives are filled with drama. This may occur if you overly value being a caretaker or if you are uncomfortable with genuine caring from someone who would be more fully available to reciprocate.

Another outcome of spending a lot of time with a bipolar partner may be your inability to demonstrate patience with someone facing difficult times. As an outgrowth of this attitude you may seek out new friends who appear "problem free." You may even be driven to idol worship by putting someone on a pedestal and wanting to spend a lot of time with that person. Sometimes this desire leads to a romantic involvement with the hope you might be "rescued" from your situation. Unfortunately, such a relationship is only a distraction from the real issue—your bipolar relationship.

While sometimes an affair leads to a new and healthy long-term relationship, some couples find they have little interest in each other once the mystery and intrigue of cheating is gone. Affairs usually end when the element of idealization ends, at which point one or both partners may feel traumatized by the sudden separation. Rather than risk unnecessary pain, it is better to work on your current relationship with your bipolar partner and either make it work or end it before committing to someone else. Be mindful that your perception of the new person in your life may also change after you and your bipolar mate have finally separated.

When to Leave

A relationship with a bipolar person is, in many ways, no different from any other intimate relationship—you may fall in and then out of love. Some people, because of religious convictions or other beliefs, feel it is best to tough out the relationship. They believe that once a commitment is made, it should not be destroyed. Still, many of these same people would draw the line at physical abuse. But rightly or wrongly, in today's world a lot of people believe that when you fall out of love it is best to move on—even when children are involved.

Perhaps you and you partner are fortunate that the bipolar symptoms are under control or relatively minor in intensity. But if this is not the case, confronting bipolar disorder on a daily basis can be challenging. Not everyone can handle it, and some are better equipped to handle the situation than others.

Making a Decision

If you can accept your partner's illness as a condition he never asked for and if your love is sincere (you must be honest with yourself about this), then staying in the relationship might be best for you and everyone concerned. You will have liberated yourself from the downward spiral of negative obsessions so you can concentrate on other things.

But, if you no longer love your bipolar partner, you will probably consider ending the relationship. Whether you no longer love this person because the illness has worn you out or you fell out of love for some mysterious reason, ending your bond merits serious consideration. If your partner requires a lot of attention, you may want to look into some alternative to you being the primary caregiver. Remember, when all is said and done, it is your life and your choice to make even if others disapprove. You may even still love your partner but feel the need to leave the relationship for different reasons, including:

- If you or other family members are in physical danger because of the illness
- If you have tried to make it work but are worn ragged, are on the verge of a nervous collapse, and are of no good to yourself or anyone else, then radical change may be called for—which includes breaking up
- If you have children and living with the bipolar parent is causing them deep confusion and uncertainty (especially after psychotherapy has been tried)
- If your bipolar partner continues to destroy any hope of financial security
- If your bipolar partner continues to act out manic sexual urges and you cannot tolerate unfaithfulness
- If caring for your bipolar partner has caused you to lose your job or lose close friendships and family

This list could go on, but the most important consideration is whether or not you still love your partner. However, even if the answer is yes, you still need to ask yourself if you can still have a reasonably peaceful and productive life with this person.

Finding Support

Separating from your partner does not mean that you can no longer benefit from bipolar-related support networks. You still have a lot to learn about yourself and about your relationship.

A growing number of support groups are available for the partners of people with bipolar disorder. Your local public library or hospital is a good place to start to obtain listings. You can also try the online resources listed in the Resources section. The support of people who identify with your situation can be invaluable.

WORD TO THE WISE

An Ending Isn't a Failure

Just because your relationship with your bipolar loved one ends, it does not mean it was a failure. Make a list of everything you have learned and have gained from having spent intimate time with this person. And, be mindful of not beating yourself up with hindsight about insights you lacked while still in the relationship.

If you no longer are in an intimate relationship with this bipolar person and are now "just friends," it may be time to move on with your life. Sometimes, even after a breakup, the nonbipolar person feels obligated to continue caring for the bipolar one. The two may carry on as "roommates" since the nonbipolar former mate feels wary about moving out and beginning a new life with somebody else. With all due respect, this decision seems unwise. The bipolar person still is not happy, the ex-partner who will not leave is not happy, and neither is the new person who is caught in the middle.

Empowerment Through Activism

A wide variety of worthy causes is available to help you feel vital, involved, and empowered rather than suffer the pain of being overwhelmed and defeated. Even if you must force yourself to be proactive, you will be constructively channeling your energies while connecting with others who are dealing with similar issues.

Legislative Advocacy

You can join organizations that focus on issues related to mental illness in general or those that focus specifically on the needs of people who live with bipolar disorder. As a member of such a group you can get involved in lobbying for legislation favorable to people living with mental illness. Or, you may become a fundraiser to support such advocacy. Some of these organizations work closely with legislators and representatives of pharmaceutical companies in a combined effort to make medication more affordable, and also health insurance more available and at a lower cost.

If joining an organization is not your thing, you may choose to contact your legislators to inform them of your support or opposition to a particular bill. Most of these organizations have websites where you can obtain a prewritten letter to sign, which they will then forward to your elected official. A partial list of related organizations includes:

- National Alliance for the Mentally Ill: *www.nami.org*
- Depression and Bipolar Support Alliance: *www.dbsalliance.org*
- Mental Health America: *www.nmha.org*
- American Foundation for Suicide Prevention: *www.afsp.org*
- American Psychological Association: *www.apa.org*
- American Psychiatric Association: *www.psych.org*
- National Association of Social Workers: *www.socialworkers.org*

Making Donations

If you have discretionary funds to spare, you might consider a donation to local service resources, such as a suicide prevention center, mental hospital, halfway house, or low-cost mental health clinic. You can also donate to mental health organizations and research centers.

Raising Funds

Charitable and nonprofit organizations offer many fundraising options. Besides simple direct solicitation by making phone calls, you might be encouraged to hold a fundraiser in your home. You can also socialize with friends or acquaintances who make regular donations to the cause.

Other common strategies include walk-a-thons and bike-a-thons, for which people pledge donations for your participation. Still other groups might have donation tables set up at malls or in business districts. Any of these situations present excellent opportunities for making new friends while pursuing a worthy cause. If you are well established in the business community, you might even consider contacting a few major corporations for their contributions.

Education

Be an activist by spreading the word and helping to educate the public. Through teaching others you can play an active role in reducing the stigma associated with mental illness while helping the public to better understand the realities of bipolar disorder. As a member of an advocacy organization you may become a public speaker, get involved in the planning and administration of conferences, or focus on the development of educational material. Educational activities may include speaking in libraries, schools, hospitals, senior centers, legislative meetings, and with the media.

Remember, by loving someone with bipolar disorder you face all the challenges inherent in any loving relationship. Simultaneously, you face many hurdles that are unique to living with this illness and caring for your loved one. But you also will discover that it is possible to enjoy a full and enriched relationship that provides happiness throughout your shared life. Especially important for you, your partner, and your relationship is to remain attentive to your personal care as you continue your lifelong journey together.

Resources

Organizations and Support Groups

Good general sources for information and support:

www.bipolar.com
www.bipolarcentral.com
www.bipolarworld.net
www.healthcentral.com/bipolar/support-group.html

For the partners of bipolar people

Bipolar Significant Others
www.bpso.org

Depression and Bipolar Support Alliance
www.dbsalliance.org

Depression-guide.com
www.depression-guide.com

Friendship Network
www.friendshipnetwork.org

Online meeting places for bipolar people
HealthyPlace.com
www.healthyplace.com

Hypomanic.com
www.hypomanic.com

Mixed Nuts
www.mixednuts.net

National Alliance for the Mentally Ill
www.nami.org

Pendulum Resources A good information source.
www.pendulum.org

Books

Behrman, Andy. *Electroboy: A Memoir of Mania* (New York: Random House, 2003).

Bloch, Jon P. *The Everything® Health Guide to Adult Bipolar Disorder* (Avon, MA: Adams Media).

Conner, Avery Z. *Fevers of the Mind* (Frederick, MD: PublishAmerica, 2002).

Duke, Patty. *Brilliant Madness: Living with Manic Depressive Illness* (New York: Bantam, 1993).

___. *Call Me Anna: The Autobiography of Patty Duke* (New York: Bantam, 1988).

Fawcett, Jan, Bernard Golden, and Nancy Rosenfeld. *New Hope for People with Bipolar Disorder: Your Friendly, Authoritative Guide to the Latest in Traditional and Complementary Solutions*, 2nd ed. (New York: Three Rivers Press, 2007)

Hinshaw, Stephen P. *The Years of Silence Are Past: My Father's Life with Bipolar Disorder* (Cambridge: Cambridge University Press, 2002).

Jamison, Kay Redfield. *An Unquiet Mind: A Memoir of Moods and Madness* (New York: Vintage, 1997).

___. *Touched with Fire: Manic Depressive Illness and the Artistic Temperament* (New York: Free Press, 1996).

Pollard, Marc. *In Small Doses: A Memoir about Accepting and Living with Bipolar Disorder* (Mill Valley, CA: Vision Books International, 2004).

Seligman, Martin. *Authentic Happiness* (New York: Free Press, 2002).

Shannon, Faye Joy. *Manic by Midnight* (Frederick, MD: PublishAmerica, 2000).

Simon, Lizzie. *Detour: My Bipolar Road Trip in 4-D* (New York: Washington Square Press, 2003).

Sources

Viguera, Adele C., et. al., "Risk of Recurrence in Women with Bipolar Disorder During Pregnancy: Prospective Study of Mood Stabilizer Discontinuaton," *American Journal of Psychiatry*, 164:1817–24 (December 2007)

"New ILO book explores working-time preferences in industrialized countries." *World of Work Magazine*, 52, November 2004

About the Authors

Dr. Jon P. Bloch (New Haven, CT) is professor of sociology at Southern Connecticut State University. He received his MA and PhD from Indiana University, where he wrote his dissertation on self-identity and the New Age movement. Dr. Bloch teaches courses in social psychology, intimacy patterns, and identity formation.

He has appeared on radio and TV stations in San Francisco, New York, Portland, Oregon, and Hartford and New Haven, Connecticut, including the Fox Ten O' Clock news and ABC News. Extremely well-versed in psychological, sociological, and anthropological theories and cutting-edge research on identity formation and the self, Dr. Bloch has published numerous articles in scholarly journals and is the author of several books. His scholarly publications include *New Spirituality, Self and Belonging: How New-Agers and Neo-Pagans Talk About Themselves,* and numerous scholarly journal articles.

Bernard Golden, PhD (Chicago, IL) has been a practicing psychologist for more than thirty years. Dr. Golden has also authored *Healthy Anger: How to Help Children and Teens Manage Their Anger*, *Unlock Your Creative Genius*, and *New Hope for People with Bipolar*

Disorder. In 1994 Dr. Golden founded Anger Management Education (*www.angermanagementeducation.com*).

Nancy Rosenfeld (Chicago, IL), who has bipolar disorder herself, is the author of three other books: *Unfinished Journey: From Tyranny to Freedom*, *Just As Much a Woman: Your Personal Guide to Hysterectomy and Beyond*, and *New Hope for People with Bipolar Disorder.* In 1993 Nancy founded AAA Books Unlimited, a literary agency, and is a public speaker with extensive radio and television experience.

Author's Note

This book reflects the cumulative knowledge, research, and experiences of its three contributing authors. The essential material in each case in this book is true. The authors have, however, made changes to protect all patients' identities and have also altered the identities of those who contributed personal accounts. Any readers who believe they recognize one of these patients or contributors are most assuredly mistaken. Examples of personal accounts apply to couples of any race, religion, ethnicity, and sexual orientation. Any perceived slight of specific people or organizations is unintentional.

The content and resources provided in this book are solely the opinion of the authors and are not intended as a substitute for therapy or professional advice. If expert advice or counseling is needed, services of a competent professional should be sought. Neither the author nor the publisher assumes any responsibility or liability whatsoever on the behalf of any purchaser or reader of these self help materials, nor do they assume any responsibility for errors, omissions, or contrary interpretations of the subject matter herein.

Index

R

S